104 ACTIVITIES THAT BUILD:
SELF-ESTEEM, TEAMWORK, COMMUNICATION, ANGER MANAGEMENT, SELF-DISCOVERY AND COPING SKILLS

BY ALANNA JONES

Rec Room Publishing, Inc.

PO Box 2117
Lusby, MD 20657
1-888-325-GAME

Library of Congress Catalog Card Number: 98-91212
ISBN-13: 978-0-9662341-3-8
ISBN-10: 0-9662341-3-8

To my son Corbin who continually shows
me the joy that comes from games and play and
who makes the game of life more fun to live!

Acknowledgments

A special thanks to Roberta Ellis and Jana Strange for all their ideas and input and for their willingness in helping me try out new games.

To Dr. Noel Gill and to Patty for their great game ideas.

A big thanks to all the creative, innovative people who attended my TAG (Therapeutic Activities and Games) workshops and who gave me ideas and inspiration for a number of games found in this book.

CONTENTS

Disclaimer

The games in this book are designed to be fun and interactive. Common sense should be used when leading and or participating in these games, and safety for all those involved should always be considered. The author and publisher are not responsible for any actions taken by any person/s who leads and/or participates in any of the games or activities in this book.

So, have fun, be safe, know the limits of the members of your group, and always give people the choice of participation to insure a good time for all!

INTRODUCTION

Teaching, learning, growing and changing by playing games? Is this possible? If you play the games and do the activities that are found in this book, you will find the answer to this question and at the same time you will find yourself having lots of fun!

Games are powerful tools that can be used in therapy, and of course games are fun. People use different tools to build a house, fix a car, cultivate a garden or to make something old look new. In therapy tools are needed to build a team out of a group of people who are working together, to help individuals who feel stuck in their old ways renew life, and to help a person grow emotionally into a better person. Games in therapy can also help people look at the problems they are dealing with through a different perspective (the activity) so they can heal and live a healthy, full life.

Games have therapeutic value in themselves – the reason people who are depressed are encouraged to engage in activities and why people at a fair or carnival are smiling and having a good time. Families are encouraged to build better relationships with each other by playing together and by participating in games that are enjoyable and fun for all. Think about your own life and the things that you do that are fun and enjoyable. How do these activities make you feel and how do they help you in your daily life? The answer to this question should be that the fun games you play and activities that you enjoy help you feel better, both emotionally and physically (otherwise you would chose to do something else during your free time). Games get you involved with other people, build relationships among individuals, make everyone equal and most of all promote laughter to help people have a good time. If you don't have any activities in your own life that bring you this kind of feeling, perhaps you need to incorporate more time into your life where you are engaged in pleasurable, healthy, fun activities. Since you bought this book, the likelihood is that you already know that games have a natural therapeutic value and you want to learn more about how to enhance that value when using these games with the group/s or individual people you wish to help.

When a game is used as a therapeutic tool, it should focus on specific goals or objectives, plus do all of the things mentioned above. When a game has a goal of improving teamwork, self-esteem, coping skills, etc. the game can be focused in a new therapeutic direction and thereby enhance the learning for all those involved. One game can focus on many different goals at a time or a single game can be altered so that the goal for the game is different each time it is played.

The discussion that takes place during a game or afterwards is the most important element in a therapeutic game. The discussion can turn an ordinary game into a therapeutic learning experience by focusing on goals, behavior and observations from the game. THE BIG WIND BLOWS (page 208) is a game in the self-discovery section that is a good example of a simple game that can be changed into a therapeutic learning experience by simply discussing the things that occurred during the game. This game is also a good example of a game that can be altered many times to create a goal centered activity that can help people focus on the treatment issues that they are working on.

In the game THE BIG WIND BLOWS everyone stands on a separate piece of paper in a circle. One person stands in the middle of the circle and says something that is true about him/herself. Everyone else must listen to what is said; and if this statement applies to them and they are standing in the circle, then each person it is true for must find a different spot to stand on that has been vacated by someone else. The person left in the middle must then say the next thing (see game instructions for further details). This is a popular game that isn't usually thought of as having therapeutic goals. By watching what goes on during the game, the leader and/or the participants can make different observations, and give people the opportunity to learn about themselves and about others in the group. Some examples of issues that arise out of this simple game are: how differences and similarities are found in the group, who likes to be the center of attention and who shies away from it, appropriate social skills and comments, cheating issues, self-esteem (not putting down others or not being afraid to say what you like), taking risk, listening skills, and physical exercise. This game also makes people laugh and feel more comfortable around one another, and it breaks up groups and gets people away from their comfort zone. All of these things can be focused on during a group discussion that takes place after the game (or sometimes during). Without a discussion these important moments of discovery would be overlooked and the chance for people to learn more from this game would be lost.

By simply changing the directions to the game THE BIG WIND BLOWS, the goals, objectives and therapeutic focus can change from game to game (see game directions for examples of how to change it). One variation can be a self-esteem activity, another an anger management game and the next time a risk taking activity to build trust among group members.

The games in this book are written in a such a way that each game is designed to focus on specific goals and objectives and are designed to be therapeutic tools when used with the discussion prompts or with a learning based discussion during or after each game. Some activities have the discussion built into the game itself and no further discussion is needed.

Every game is designed to be therapeutic and to give individuals the chance to share their thoughts and feelings in a non-threatening way. Each activity also gives people the chance to practice improving their behavior during the course of the game and to learn new skills that can be taken and applied to the real world. Each person will respond to the games differently; by using a wide variety of games that address different issues, there will be more of a chance for each unique individual to learn and to discover new things about him/herself.

SELECTING THE GAME

Choosing which game will meet the needs of a specific group or individual is the first step when preparing a therapeutic game session. Start by focusing on the obvious issues faced by the group members and set your group goals accordingly. If after assessing a group, you find there is a strong need for anger management, then your goal may be to find games that focus on that topic. Just because you find that a group has a strong need to work on some very specific issues, don't overlook the other areas such as self-esteem, communication skills, etc. By learning various life skills and by working on a variety of goals, each of the group member's needs can be addressed. Often a game will reveal a need that was not originally seen as a priority when an original thorough assessment was completed.

Besides knowing the issues your group needs to work on, you should have a wide variety of resources available to you when selecting a game. Books, other people, and your past experiences are the best resources you have, so use them all! There are some really great activities out there but be aware, some activities have been used so often that it is almost impossible to find a person who hasn't done the activity before, especially when you work with people who have been through a variety of treatment type programs. If you try new things, the therapeutic value will be stronger because it is more likely that nobody has played the game before. Hopefully this book will give you some good ideas that you can use and if you like the games in this book, you will also find *The wRECking Yard of Games and Activities* helpful as well. When thinking of games, think of what you played as a child or even games you like now, and often times these games can be adapted to create a new therapeutic game by changing the game slightly or adding a discussion, and before you know it you will have a new game that focuses on specific goals, objectives, and issues.

LEADiNG THE GAME

Once you have selected a game and developed your goals for the group, it is time to play and have fun! When leading a game you may either participate yourself or you may simply lead and allow the group to play by themselves while you observe. If one of your goals is to build rapport between yourself and the group members, whenever possible you should be involved in the game. By being a part of the group you can build relationships and trust as well as have a good time. For some people the games involve taking a personal risk by stepping out of one's comfort zone and being willing to participate, share feelings, or accept feedback from others. The more willing the leader is to take a risk the more willing group members are to step out of their individual comfort zones and join in the activity. "Challenging" people to participate rather than stating they "have to" is a good way to create a non-threatening atmosphere and to empower people with the power of choice. Remind people that therapy is about growing and stretching emotionally so that they can overcome obstacles, and that stepping out of one's comfort zone and trying new things is the best way for them to grow and to change their lives for the better.

There are times when it is best to get the game started and then to step back and act as an observer while the group members participate in the activity. This is especially true for teamwork activities. When a group of people are given a challenging task and the leader is participating, they will often look to the leader for guidance and suddenly the group is unable to work to its full potential. By allowing a group to work on its own in this type of situation, the leader empowers the group members, and individuals are able to step forward and have a bigger role in the group than they would if the leader were involved in the activity.

THE THERAPEUTIC DISCUSSION

As mentioned before, the discussion is a key element in any therapeutic game or activity. Getting people to think about what they have just done during a game is a powerful way for them to learn about themselves. One of most effective ways to use games in therapy is to point out behaviors as they occur rather than waiting for a later discussion or group time to talk about past behaviors. When a person is given the opportunity to work on his/her behaviors as they are occurring, there is more opportunity for change, growth and improvement in existing behaviors. A discussion can help people understand better what it is that they are doing and what it is that needs to change. It can also be a chance for other group members and leaders to point out improvements that have been made so individuals can see progress in their own treatment.

A discussion can take on many different forms and should be adapted to the level of the group. A higher functioning group may sit in a circle where everyone gives input and answers any questions posed to them after the activity. A lower functioning group may simply raise their hands in response to yes and no questions. The discussion should debrief what just happened and then be made applicable to the group members' lives. For example, when working on teamwork you may discuss what happened, the roles different people took on in the activity and compare this with how the participants respond when in other groups where they must work as a team member such as in the family, when on a sports team, at work, or in a variety of relationships.

The discussion prompts at the end of each game are meant to be a guide and to give you focus for the goals of the activity. These questions are a helpful guide but the reality of a therapeutic session is that you address what comes up and sometimes the topics cannot be predicted ahead of time. If you start the discussion by simply asking the group members if they had any observations during the game, the discussion will then take on a life of its own and address behaviors that you may not have observed. Encourage participants to focus on their own behaviors and issues and on how their actions can be improved or how they affect others. Sometimes the discussion won't be about what actually happened during a game but about how the game is like life. In an anger management game you may discuss how people deal with things that are "unfair" after playing a game with unfair rules and relate this to their actions of anger when they are in an unfair situation. This is just another way that games can be a powerful tool in therapy!

This book is meant to give you ideas, plans for therapeutic groups and to spark your imagination so you can create more therapeutic games. It can also be useful for camp, church groups, scouts or whatever other group with which you may work. Don't forget to have fun, laugh and enjoy yourself while in the process of helping others learn more about themselves and the world around them.

TEAMWORK

Teamwork activities are fun to lead, exciting to participate in, challenging, and almost always the favorite type of therapeutic games to play. One teamwork activity can cover a wide variety of issues and address a large number of goals - all at the same time. A simple game can tackle social skills, communication and anger management while building self-esteem, group cohesiveness, rapport, and validating each person in the group. Even though all the things mentioned above (plus many more) can be seen in a teamwork activity, it is often not apparent until a group gathers for discussion what all the different issues were that arose during the course of the activity.

As the leader of countless teamwork activities, I have learned to sit back and be very observant while a group is engaged in the challenge I have set before them. During the discussion I ask the group to tell me what it is that they observed about themselves and about the group as a whole during the activity and then I will fill in the gaps with my observations about what occurred.

Without even knowing a group of people, I can put a teamwork challenge before them and by watching learn who is a dominant leader, who is passive, shy, or who has a low self-esteem. Also I can see who is afraid of rejection, who tries to assert power over others, who is a good leader, etc. by observing the group skills of people found in a diverse group. All this can come from one simple game, and when the group dynamics are brought up in a discussion, a fun game quickly becomes a powerful tool for people to learn about themselves and to learn about how they relate to others. These lessons can then be applied to the lives of the people in the group by asking the group, "What skills do you need if you are to be successful in a teamwork situation?" and "When in life will you need to use these skills?". There are so many areas in life in which teamwork skills are important such as working, playing sports, doing school projects, getting along with others - a friend, spouse, parent, child or any other family member.

Teamwork activities not only cover a wide variety of topics but also come in many different forms. The most popular form of teamwork activities are outdoor adventure programs, which are powerful and effective. The reality is that not every therapist, counselor or teacher has the means or the budget to offer this type of therapeutic program, so that's where the games in this book can be useful. Many of the games can be done with very limited resources, time and space if needed. Hopefully you will find that a wide variety of these games can be useful, adaptable, or be helpful for the population with which you work.

TEAMWORK GAMES AND ACTIVITIES

CREATE A COUNTRY

When the founding fathers of the United States of America first got together to form a government, they had many issues to agree on and many decisions to make. I'm sure discussion, compromise, problem solving and teamwork were a large part of the process when they tackled the tough task of forming a government. Creating a country wouldn't be an easy task, but in this activity it can be fun when the group pulls together and uses teamwork to solve the problems they face.

Objective
For people to get together as a group and participate in a group decision making process.

Who
People who need to learn to work with others as a member of a group when the group must make decisions together.

Group Size
2 or more

Materials
- Paper
- Pens or pencils
- Colored markers, colored pencils or crayons

Description
Divide the group into smaller groups of two to ten members each. Provide each group with the following information and all of the materials listed above.

"You and a group of people have claimed an uninhabited island as a new country. You have been selected to be the new government. Your first assignment is to make the following decisions and accomplish the following tasks...

1. Name the country

2. Nickname of the country

3. Design a license plate

4. Design a flag

5. Choose a national bird

6. Choose a national flower

7. Write a national anthem

8. Appoint yourselves to government offices

9. Create any laws that you feel are necessary

10. In addition to your government appointment each person must pick a job serving the needs of the country"

The group must work together to complete the task and then present it to the leaders or to the rest of the group when finished. This activity may take more than one session to complete or you may wish to have the group simply select the things from the list that they can complete in the time given to them.

Discussion Prompts

1. How were decisions made in your group?

2. Is everyone happy with what was decided? Why or why not?

3. What things are important to remember when making group decisions?

4. What role do you usually take when making decisions with others?

5. How can you tell if a group has been successful when making a decision?

6. Why is it important to be able to make decisions as a member of a group?

GARBAGE ART

Creating a piece of art is an easy task for one person because his/her creativity, ideas and visions can be put into a single piece of art. When more than one person works on a piece of art all the different ideas must come together in agreement so that in the end the team creates a single piece of wonderfully creative art.

Objective
For a group of people to make decisions together, work together and to create a piece of art together.

Who
People who need to learn how to work with others on a group project by practicing making decisions and communicating with others.

Group Size
2 or more

Materials
- Scissors
- Glue
- Tape
- Any garbage item that can be used for art. Some suggestions are...toilet paper/paper towel rolls, egg cartons, milk cartons, foil, pop cans, can lids, newspaper, string, and anything else you can find!

Description
Collect anything that can be used to create a piece of "art" or "sculpture" (see materials for suggestions). Place all of the items in a pile so that group members may select items to be used in their sculpture. It is a good idea to have two to four people working on one

piece of art and to have groups take turns selecting items from the pile. You may wish to give each group glue, tape and scissors.

Allow time for the groups to create their "garbage art". When everyone is finished with their project, allow time for an art gallery exhibit and let each group display their own piece of art, share what it is, and tell any story they have about it.

Discussion Prompts

1. How did you and the other members of your group decide which pieces of garbage to use?
2. How did you decide what to build?
3. Was everyone included in the decision process? If not, why? If so, how?
4. What unique thing did each person in the group contribute to the project?
5. Why is it important to be able to work on group projects with other people?

CREATIVE COLORING

Sometimes in life we must accept help from others or rely on our friends and family for help if we are to be successful. If one person tries to build a house all alone, there is a lot of work to be done and it's a difficult task, but when a whole team of people pitch in and contribute, a complete house can be built in no time. Each person is a part of a puzzle and can offer different talents to use in the building of the complete house.

In this activity each person is a part of a team that can make a big project easy and each person contributes his/her own skills to create the big picture.

Objective
For each person to contribute to a group project and for the group to work together as a team.

Who
People who need to practice using teamwork by working closely with others to finish a group project.

Group Size
4 to 12 participants

Materials
- ➲ 12 different colored markers, crayons or colored pencils
- ➲ A large sheet of paper

Description
Give each member of the group a different colored marker, crayon or pencil and inform them that this will be the only color they can use for this project. The group must now create a picture, using all of the

colors. Each person may only use his/her color (no trading or sharing is allowed!).

For example if the picture contains a tree the person with the brown marker will draw the tree trunk and the person with the green will then draw the leaves.

Discussion Prompts

1. Was this a difficult task for the group? Why or why not?
2. How did you work as group to complete the picture?
3. Is everyone in the group happy with the picture that was created? Why or why not?
4. Is it easier to do things by yourself or with others?
5. Why is it important to be able to work with others as a member of a team?

Variations

- ⊃ For smaller groups each person may have more than one color.
- ⊃ For younger children or lower functioning groups it's a good idea to tell them what picture they should draw.
- ⊃ Have the group color in a page from a coloring book, rather than creating their own picture.
- ⊃ For added teamwork ask the group to decide how to determine which color each person will use.

BiG SHOES

When a group works together as a team, each person has the opportunity to help the others, so that the team can be successful in the end. If one person on a team doesn't contribute, then the rest of the team must work harder to make up for the one person who is slacking. At other times if one person doesn't help the team, then the team cannot succeed no matter how hard the others are trying, and the group will not be able to finish the task that they have set out to do. This activity requires that all the people involved contribute to the team or the team will not be able to accomplish the fun but difficult task.

Objective
To work together as a team in order to accomplish a challenging activity.

Who
People who need to be able to work with others in a teamwork situation.

Group Size
2 to 4 participants (or split a large group into small groups of 2 to 4 each)

Materials
- Two 2"x4"x6' boards
- 2 to 4 pairs of large old shoes

Description
Gather together two to four pairs of old shoes that are rather large in size. Firmly attach the soles of the shoes (with nails, screws or strong glue) to the boards in such a manner that they all face the same way and one shoe from each pair is on each board across from its mate.

Place the "big shoes" at one end of a large area and ask the participants to put their feet in the shoes. Give the group the challenge of moving as a unit across the large area to reach the other end successfully.

Discussion Prompts

1. What did the group have to do during this activity in order to be successful?
2. What role did you take in this activity?
3. Are there ever times in your life when you must work together with others to accomplish a goal? If so, when and what do you do to contribute?

Variations

➲ With a large group, take turns using the "Big Shoes" or make more than one set for the group.
➲ Use a timer so the group may do it more than once and attempt to beat their own time.

BiD AND BUiLD

Deciding how to spend money can create many problems and much tension among family members, company executives, or any other group that works with money. When money is scarce and hard to come by, the decisions must be made carefully and input should be given from all those who are involved.

Objective
To problem solve and to make group decisions as a team.

Who
People who need practice being part of a group decision making process.

Group Size
4 to 20 participants

Materials
- ➲ A large sheet of paper, chalkboard, dry erase board, etc.
- ➲ A writing utensil for the paper, chalkboard, or dry erase board
- ➲ Various items that can be used or not used to get a group from point A to point B (i.e. Frisbees®, sheets of paper, rope, hula hoops, pieces of wood or cardboard, an old garbage can, a tumbling mat and anything else you can find.)
- ➲ Paper
- ➲ Pens or pencils
- ➲ Optional: Play money

Description
This activity is two teamwork activities in one! For the first part, list all the items that you have gathered on the large sheet of paper, display it for the group to see, and show them the items listed. Divide the group into at least two smaller groups of two or more and give each group a piece of paper and a pen or pencil. Explain to the groups that

their task is to attempt to get their entire team from one side of an open area to the other side (at least ten yards apart) using any of the items listed and without anyone on their team touching the ground at any time.

First the teams must bid for the items listed. Each team gets 100 points (or $100 in play money) that they may spend however they wish on the items. They must divide up the points based on what they think will help them the most and write down their bids on the paper given to them. For example one team may bid 75 points on the Frisbees, and 25 points on the rope. Another team may bid 50 points on the rope and 25 points on the Frisbees and another 10 on the paper and 15 on the cardboard.

After all the bids are completed, collect them and divide up the materials based upon the highest bid. So the first team would end up with the Frisbees and nothing else but the second team would get the rope, paper and cardboard. If there is a tie for any item you may have the teams bid again on certain items or divide up the items if possible.

Once the teams have their items the second part of this teamwork activity occurs. They must now work as a team to successfully get their entire team across the open area without any of the team members touching the ground in the process.

Discussion Prompts
1. Was it hard for your team to agree on what numbers to bid? Why or why not?
2. What did you do to come to an agreement?
3. When you disagree with others how do you handle it?
4. How do you feel about your ability to work with others after this activity?
5. What role do you usually take when in a group that is making decisions? Do you feel this is a good role or a bad role for you? Why?

Variation
➲ This activity may be done for an art project as well. Teams must bid on items that can be used to create a piece of art.

BUBBLE BRIGADE

When trying to solve a problem or to come up with the answer to a tough question, a group (or person) is not challenged if the answer comes easy. When people must try again and again before they successfully come up with an answer to a tough question, the more exciting and fun it is to finally find the answer.

Even something as simple as making bubbles can become a whole new exciting adventure when the task at hand is challenging and the group must work together, be resourceful, and ultimately find the answer.

Objective
To work together with others as a member of a group. To problem solve and attempt to solve a challenging task as a group.

Who
People who have the ability to problem solve, but who need to work on using their teamwork skills when solving a problem with a group.

Group Size
2 to 4 participants (or split a large group into small groups of 2 to 4 each)

Materials
- Bowl
- Liquid soap or dish soap
- Water
- Drinking Straws
- Yarn

Description

Give the group all the supplies and explain to them that their task is to make bubbles (that float in the air) out of what you have given them. Also challenge them to make the biggest bubble possible.

Hint: The soap and water can be mixed to make a weak bubble solution, so just making a bubble is a challenge but mixing it right makes it easier. The string and yarn may be used to make bubbles by putting a piece of string through two straws and tying it in a loop so that it makes a square when you are done. Then hold the straws and dip it in the bubble mix and try to create a bubble. You may want to cut the straws in half to make smaller bubble makers. Or simply use your fingers to make a circle that can be used to create bubbles.

Discussion Prompts

1. Was this task frustrating for anyone in the group? If so, why? If not, why?
2. How did the group come up with a solution?
3. Was it necessary to work with others to accomplish this task? Why or why not?
4. How did working with others make the process of problem solving easier? Or did it make it more difficult for you?
5. What did you do to contribute to the group?
6. How did you feel about your contribution?

PEOPLE TREE

Climbing a tree is something that many people have done at least once in their life. Some trees are easier to climb than others, but when a group of people climb a tree, a tree that was once an easy climb may become more challenging. When some of the group members have injuries or a disability then the task is even more challenging.

The challenge in this activity occurs when the group must think of safety first (of course picking a safe tree helps) and they must think of others before themselves. Creating a plan of action before starting up the tree is a good idea as well. Have fun but don't forget, what goes up must come down!

Objective
For a group to work together to accomplish a task and to keep everyone safe in the process.

Who
People who need to work on teamwork skills but who have the ability to act in a safe manner and who can be helpful to others.

Group Size
3 or more (depending on size of tree)

Materials
- A good safe climbing tree
- A cup filled with water (optional)

Description
Find a good climbing tree. Give the group the challenge of getting everyone into the tree (you may need to put a restriction on how high they can go). Don't go beyond the limits of your group and be sure that safety is a factor when doing this activity (helmets, people observing

others for safety, and a tree with wide low hanging branches are recommended)!

To make the activity more challenging you may want to designate a few of the group members as "injured", or "disabled" giving them an injury to act out while attempting to climb the tree (i.e. blind, broken arm, broken leg, etc.). To add another challenge, give the group a cup of water that must be passed up the tree without being spilled.

Discussion Prompts

1. How did the group work together to get everyone into the tree? Were there any problems?
2. Would it have been possible to do this activity without talking? Why or why not?
3. How was teamwork a factor in this activity?
4. How did the group members help each other?
5. Do you ever need help from others or find yourself in a position to help others? When, and in what situations?

STRAW TOWER

This is a challenging activity that involves creativity, and there are many, many solutions to the problem. The real challenge occurs when one group of people must work together with many different ideas and possible solutions to solve one problem when only one answer may be given from each team.

Objective
To show teamwork by working with others to complete a task and by being involved in a group decision making process.

Who
People who need to learn to accept others ideas, give their own ideas and come up with a compromise in the end.

Group Size
2 to 10 participants

Materials
- Drinking straws
- Paper clips
- String
- Pipe cleaners
- Scissors

Description
Provide the group with a pile of straws, paper clips, pipe cleaners, scissors and a ball of string. Inform the group that their task is to use the materials that they have been given to build a tower that is as tall as possible without it falling over. Give the group a time limit to complete the task.

For added incentive have more than one team and challenge them to build the tallest tower.

Discussion Prompts

1. How did your group get started with this project?
2. Did everyone agree on how the tower should be built? If not, how was a decision made?
3. What part did you take in the decision making?
4. Do you usually follow what others say or do you attempt to get others to do what you want? Why? What is usually the end result of this process?
5. What are some good ways for a group of people to make decisions together?
6. Why is it important for you to be able to work with others and to make decisions as a member of a group?

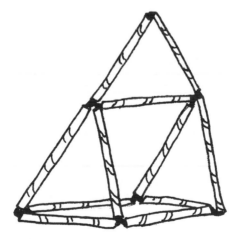

SCAVENGER HUNT SWITCH

Scavenger hunts have been around for a long time. The usual list consist of everyday items, and a few odd ones, that can be found in someone's home. Coming up with a creative and challenging list takes time, but the more people there are working on the list and giving input, the easier it is to create a great scavenger hunt.

Objective
To make decisions as a group and to work together on a team project.

Who
People who need practice working with others when making group decisions.

Group Size
6 or more

Materials
- ⇒ Paper
- ⇒ Pens or pencils
- ⇒ Large paper bags

Description
Divide the group into teams with three or more people on each team. Supply each team with a piece of paper and a pen or pencil. Instruct each team to make a list of ten items that could be found on a scavenger hunt, in a designated area. Some typical items found on a list are… a five pointed leaf, a penny older than ten years, an old pop can (lists will vary depending on the area you choose for the scavenger hunt to take place). Once each team has made up their lists, collect them and redistribute them among the teams. Each group must then attempt to

collect all the items on the list they have been given before the allotted time is up.

At the end of the time limit gather the teams back together so they can each show the other groups all of the items that they were able to collect from their list.

Discussion Prompts

1. Did everyone on your team give input when making the list?
2. What role did each person from your team take on during this activity?
3. Why is it important to be able to make decisions when in a group situation?
4. What can you do to help a group make decisions easily?

Variations

➲ Add competition by giving points for each item found or give bonus points to the team that finds all of the items in the quickest amount of time.
➲ Do a treasure hunt switch instead with clues placed around a specific area by different teams.

NUMBERS VOLLEYBALL

Volleyball is a popular team sport, but if you play on some teams it seems more like an individual sport. Some people dominate the game and don't allow others to hit the ball (even people on their own team)! In this game it's the teamwork that counts. Hitting the ball more than once on a side takes more than one person and lots of teamwork. What matters is the teamwork and the team that works together the most will be the team that wins in the end.

Objective
To work together with others to reach a group goal.

Who
People who like to play volleyball but who always hog the ball and hit it over the net, instead of using teamwork to get the ball over the net.

Group Size
6 to 20 participants

Materials
- ➲ Volleyball net
- ➲ Beach ball or Volleyball
- ➲ Pen, Paper and envelope or small container

Description
Prior to the activity cut a piece of paper into six pieces and number each piece with a different number, 1 through 6. Place these slips of paper into an envelope or small container.

Divide the group into two equal teams with one team on each side of the volleyball net. Play volleyball by the regular rules with a beach ball or volleyball. Prior to each serve select a number from the envelope. This number indicates the number of times the ball <u>must</u> be hit by members of a team on its side before the ball is returned to the other side of the net. For example, if the number 5 is chosen, each team must hit the ball exactly 5 times before returning it to the other team. If the ball is hit more or less than 5 times then the other team gains the serve or earns a point. Prior to each serve draw a new number and play until one team reaches 15 points.

Discussion Prompts
1. Did you have to use more or less teamwork for this game than in a regular volleyball game?
2. What did your team have to do in order to be successful at this activity?
3. Why is teamwork important?
4. What happens if an individual on your team doesn't use teamwork?
5. What are some qualities of a good team?

GROUP TRANSFORMATION

When you go to a sporting event that has cheerleaders you will notice that there is usually a whole team of cheerleaders and rarely is there just one. One cheerleader can get the fans to yell and to be motivated to cheer for their team, but a whole group can build pyramids, perform dances and entertain a crowd.

This activity can be done by one person, but it takes a whole team to accomplish the task and complete the challenge. A group must work together to create sculptures and objects using only their bodies. Of course teamwork and togetherness are the most important elements needed for the success of this activity.

Objective
To work as a team to a create group sculpture that includes everyone in the group.

Who
People who need to learn to work with others as a part of a team. People who can be in close proximity with one another.

Group Size
4 or more

Materials
➲ None

Description
Create a list of objects that a group can create a sculpture of using only their bodies. Each sculpture must include everyone in the group and may be moving or still. Some sculpture ideas are typewriter, computer, semi-truck, bulldozer, sink, helicopter, food processor, shower, etc. If this is done in teams there is more incentive for each

group to work quickly and efficiently in response to the added competition of others. You may wish to have a time limit in which the sculpture must be created and give points to teams that do it quickly.

Discussion Prompts

1. Did everyone feel included in this activity? Why or why not?
2. How did you decide who did what in your group?
3. How do you usually make decisions when with a group? Is this a good or bad way? Why?
4. What are some good ways to make decisions as a group?

CUP STACK

This activity has been a strong favorite at the Therapeutic Activities and Games Workshops that have been held around the country. Some groups complete the task very quickly while other groups must keep trying and trying to complete the task successfully. The hardest part is not giving up when things get tough or frustrating or more importantly not to cheat (I've seen plenty of that at the workshops too)! Either way it's always a favorite and a fun activity.

Objective
To work together to accomplish a difficult task without quitting or giving up when someone gets frustrated.

Who
People who have difficulty working with others but who need the practice in order to improve their social skills. People who give up easily.

Group Size
3 or more (ideal to have groups of 6)

Materials
- ➲ Scissors
  FOR EACH GROUP:
- ➲ 10 paper cups of equal size
- ➲ One rubber band (must fit around a cup)
- ➲ 6 pieces of string (two to three feet long each)

Description
(Prior to the activity cut six pieces of string, into two to three foot long pieces for each group.) Tie each piece to a rubber band as evenly spaced as possible so you finish with a rubber band with six pieces of string attached to it (it should look like a sunshine with six sun rays

going out in all directions). Make one of these for every six people.

Divide your group into smaller groups of six (or as close to this as possible). Give each group a stack of ten paper cups and one of the rubber band/string implements that you have prepared. Place the paper cups on the table, spread out and upside down.

Challenge the group to build a pyramid out of the paper cups (four on the bottom, three on the next row, then two, and finally one on the top). Group members may not touch the cups with their hands, or any other part of their bodies for that matter, even if a cup falls on the floor.

Each person should hold onto one of the strings that are attached to the rubber band and the group then uses this device to pick up the cups and place them on top of each other (by pulling the rubber band apart and then bringing it back together over the cups). If there are less than six people on any given team, some team members may have to hold more than one string (but this does make it a bit easier).

Discussion Prompts

1. Was anyone frustrated at all during this activity? If so how was it handled?
2. Why was teamwork so important for this activity?
3. Are you ever in a situation where you must use teamwork? Is this always easy for you? Why or why not?
4. What are some skills needed to be good at teamwork?
5. What is so hard about teamwork?
6. What did you do today to contribute to the teamwork on your team?

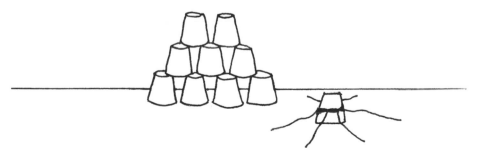

VOLLEY HOOP

Some people who are good athletes (or who think that they are good athletes) tend to be "ball hogs" when ever they play a game. They get in front of other people who are on their own team and intercept the ball or they never pass the ball to anyone and keep it for themselves. This leaves others feeling left out, frustrated and discouraged about playing the game. When everyone has an equal part in a game, it can be much more fun for everyone and gives the "ball hogs" a chance to experience what good teamwork really is.

Objective
To be aware of the other people on your team and to show this through the use of communication.

Who
People who have difficulty thinking of others when on a team and who could benefit from practicing being an equal part of a team, rather than the dominant member of a team.

Group Size
8 to 12 is ideal

Materials
- Volleyball net
- Beach ball
- 4 more hula hoops than players (or string or tape to make circles on the ground)

Description
Set up the volleyball net as you would for a regular volleyball game and divide the group into two equal teams. Place the hula hoops (or what ever you use to make circles) on the ground on each side, spread

out. There should be two more circles than they are players on each side. Ask each team to go to its side and each person to select a hula hoop to stand in. One team serves the beach ball to begin the game.

During the game everyone must be in a hula hoop at all times, but only one person may occupy a given hula hoop at a time. During the game any player may move to an unoccupied hoop to help his/her team get the ball over the net. Play as you would for a regular beach ball volleyball game, but you may wish to allow more than three hits per side to start. There is lots of teamwork involved in a game where people must share the court with their teammates!

Discussion Prompts

1. Did you have to use communication in this game?
2. Is communication important for teamwork? Why?
3. Did you have to think about your teammates more or less in this game than in regular volleyball? Why?
4. How did your team do at using teamwork? What did it do?
5. How did you do at using teamwork? What did you do?

CANDY REACH

A piñata, Easter egg hunt, and trick-or-treat; these are all great ways to get candy, but it's every man for himself! People can become super competitive when there is candy involved, but in this game the more teamwork used the more candy you get!

Objective
To work together with your partner to problem solve and help each other to reach your goal.

Who
People who need practice working together with a partner to problem solve and who need practice offering help to others and accepting help from others. People must be able to be in a close space with other people.

Group Size
2 or more

Materials
- ➲ An assorted bag of individually wrapped candy
- ➲ A piece of cardboard, wood, carpet scrap etc. that is big enough for two people to stand on at the same time

Description
Set up the game prior to the activity by placing the board on the floor (make sure it won't slide - maybe tape it down) and spreading the candy on the floor, all around the board. Put the pieces of candy far enough away that they would be hard to reach if you were standing on the board by yourself.

Ask the group to get into pairs. Challenge each pair to take a turn trying to get as much of the candy as they can by working with their partner and state the following rules.

1. *Both you and your partner must be on the board at all times*
2. *No part of your body or clothing may touch the floor at any time*
3. *If you touch the floor you must go to the end of the line before trying again*
4. *You may not slide the cardboard*
5. *You must pick up the candy, not drag it*
6. *You may not use anything (i.e. belt, piece of clothing) to pick up the candy*
7. *What ever candy you pick up you and your partner may keep*
8. *Once you pick up one piece you may only try for ten more seconds before you go to the end of the line*

Rule number eight is in place because once a team figures out a good way to get candy they may be able to get every single piece. You may wish to allow this and replenish the supply for each pair. It is a good idea to put some really good pieces of candy really far away to add to the challenge. Also for a shorter or taller pair you may need to adjust the distance of the board according to the group. To emphasize teamwork allow time for groups to come up with a plan and to practice before trying it out on the candy.

Hint: One person holds the other person who reaches out to get the candy.

Discussion Prompts

1. What did you and your partner have to do to be successful at this activity?
2. Could you have done this alone? Why or why not?
3. Are you ever in a situation where you must rely on others to be successful? Are you able to accept help from others? Why or why not?
4. When would it be good for you to accept help from others? Can you?

ONE BODY

Each person in every group of people is unique and each person can add a special element to the group dynamics. Sometimes people don't recognize this and they feel left out or like they don't belong.

In this activity each person contributes to the group project in his/her own small, unique way. The end result is a picture that truly belongs to everyone. It is a part of everyone in the group and can help each person feel like they contribute their own special qualities to the group to make it special.

Objective
To work together as a group to create one large picture of a body with everyone contributing to the end result.

Who
People who need to work on being a part of a group.
People who have difficulty feeling like they belong to a group or feeling like they make a difference.

Group Size
10 is ideal but 2 or more can work

Materials
➲ A large sheet of paper
➲ A black marker
➲ Colored markers, crayons, pens or pencils

Description
This activity is simple. Lay out the large sheet of paper on the ground and trace a body part from each person to create one complete body. For smaller groups use more of each body and for larger groups

you can even trace individual fingers or do more than one body. After a body has been created allow the group to color in the body and as a group create one person.

Discussion Prompts

1. How was each person able to contribute to this project?
2. Are you ever in a situation where you can contribute to a group? Do you? Why or why not?
3. Do you like to be a part of a group? Why or why not?
4. How can others in a group help you?
5. Are you willing to accept help from others? Why or why not?

FOOT BRIDGE

Solving a problem is easy when all the elements of the answer are given to you. However, when the answer must be pieced together, it suddenly becomes more difficult to solve a simple problem. It is times like this that a team of people can come together and use all their brainpower collectively to solve a problem.

With some teamwork and a bit of thinking this teamwork activity can be solved rather quickly and then the group members must help each other carry out the solution by working together.

Objective
To work together as a part of a team to problem solve and to accomplish a difficult task.

Who
People who can problem solve but who need to learn to do this with a group of people.

Group Size
4 or more

Materials
➲   10 flat boards or pieces of cardboard (about 1' x 1' or a bit larger)

Description
Explain to the group that they will have to get their group from one end of the room to the other. The rules are that they can only use the boards given to them to cross the room. They may not touch the floor at anytime while trying to cross, but may step on the boards. Once a board has been placed on the ground it may not be moved, (unless the group decides to start over and picks up all the boards). Also once someone steps on a board they may move forward but never backwards.

At this point divide the group in half and give each small group five boards (or enough boards to get half way across the room but no further when laying them down and stepping on them to create a "bridge"). Explain that this needs to be done in smaller groups so you must divide them. Place one group on one side of the room and the other group as far away from the first group as you can on the opposite side of the room (but facing each other). Ask them to devise a plan that will get their small group across the room while observing all the rules.

At this point both groups will try to get across which is very difficult because they don't have enough boards to make a bridge unless they figure out that the two opposite teams must meet in the middle and help each other to create one large bridge. Due to the fact that you can not go backwards there will be some teamwork needed to get around each other in the middle when teams are going in opposite directions.

This is a fun one and the less hints you give them the better and the further apart the teams are, the more effective the game!

Discussion Prompts

1. What was needed from both groups in order for this activity to be successful?
2. How did you feel when you had to cross paths with the other team in the middle of the bridge?
3. Are there ever times in your life when you must rely on others in order to be successful at something? When and what do you do?
4. Is it ever hard for you to ask others for help? Why?
5. When should you ask others for help? Do you?

TEAM SCORE BASKETBALL

When playing basketball there are always a few people who score most of the baskets for each team. When the score is determined by how much teamwork is used instead of by how many points are scored, then everyone is involved in making the baskets, rather than one person taking all the glory for him/herself.

Objective
To use every member of your team to accomplish a group goal.

Who
People who need to work on using teamwork when in a competitive situation.

Group Size
6 to 10 is ideal

Materials
◗ Basketball
◗ Basketball Court

Description
Divide the group into two teams as you would for a normal basketball game and play basketball by normal rules. However, in order to win this game each and every person on your team must score one basket, and no more.

If the game goes quickly, change the rules so a point is scored each time every person on a team successfully scores a basket.

Discussion Prompts

1. How was this different from a normal basketball game? How was your participation different?
2. Was this harder or easier and why?
3. Were you frustrated if someone else on your team had a hard time making a basket? If so, how did you deal with this frustration?
4. Is it hard sometimes to include everyone? Why or why not?
5. Do you have trouble including others; or do you often feel that you are excluded from a group?
6. Why is it important to include others?
7. How can you help to include others or include yourself in an activity?

Variation

➲ This will work for other games as well, such as soccer or hockey.

Six, Three, One

A three point shot in a basketball game will help your team more than a two point shot even though it is much harder to make. A team with a good three-point shooter has a big advantage over a team that doesn't have one.

In this game teamwork is used to make the big points. The more people who score on each team the more "three-pointers" will be made and even some "six-pointers" too!

Objective
To include everyone on your team when you play a game.

Who
People who need to practice including everyone on their team when they play a sport or competitive game.

Group Size
6 to 20 is ideal

Materials
➲ A basketball, football or soccer ball (depending on what game you decide to play)

Description
For this activity select a game that involves two teams who are going against each other to try to score points (such as Basketball, Football or Soccer). The first time an individual scores a point for his/her team, it is worth six points for the team. The second score a person makes is worth three points, and all scores after that are worth only one point each. The more people on your team who score, the more points your team receives!

Discussion Prompts

1. Did you like the rules of this game? Why or why not?
2. Was teamwork important during this game? Why?
3. Did you use everyone on your team? Why?
4. Does everyone always get to be involved in a game? Why?
5. When is it important to include everyone in an activity?
6. What are some ways you can help others to feel included?

OVER, UNDER, THROUGH

If you've ever come up against a barbed wire fence, you know that there are three ways to get to the other side (if you don't cut it). You can go over it, under it, or through the gaps.

In this game people may either go over, under or through the ropes, just as they would a barbed wire fence. Only there are a few extra rules that must be followed to add to the challenge, and of course teamwork will be the key ingredient needed for a team to be successful.

Objective
To work as a team to problem solve and to build trust and communication among group members while keeping everyone safe in the process.

Who
People who need to learn to problem solve as a group.
People who need to learn to work with others and rely on others for help. People who need to learn to be trustworthy.

Group Size
5 or more

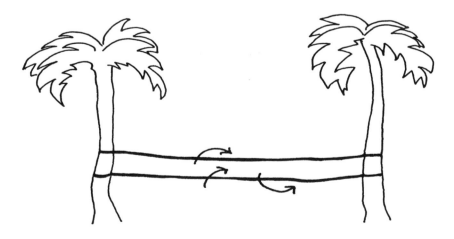

Materials
➲ 2 long ropes
➲ Something to tie the ropes between (i.e. trees, volleyball net stands)

Description
Tightly tie the two ropes horizontally between the two trees (or wherever else you find to tie them) so that there is enough room for each member of the group to get his/her body between the two ropes but so that they may need help to do so. The height of the ropes will vary depending on the functioning level of the group and the size of the group members.

Once the ropes are in place challenge the group to get all of its members from one side of the ropes to the other successfully. Then explain the following rules for the activity.

1. *No one may touch the ropes at any time, or the whole team must start over.*
2. *One person must go over the top of the highest rope*
3. *One person must go under the lowest rope*
4. *The rest of the team must go between the two ropes*
5. *You may not go around the ropes*

Emphasize safety and teamwork throughout this activity

Discussion Prompts
1. How do you think your team did at this activity?
2. What was the hardest part?
3. What did you have to do in order to be successful?
4. What role did you take on during this activity?
5. What role do you usually take when involved in a teamwork situation?
6. When in your life is teamwork an important thing?
7. What teamwork skills do you need to improve on? Which ones are you good at?

JAILBREAK

If you were to be handcuffed to someone else, a lot of teamwork would be needed to do everyday tasks, as you will see in this fun, but simple teamwork activity.

Objective
To work with a partner to accomplish a difficult task, using teamwork and communication to be successful.

Who
People who need to learn to think of others and who need to learn to use communication skills as a part of their teamwork skills.

Group Size
2 or more

Materials
- 1 piece of foot long rope for every 2 people
- Various game materials

Description
Divide the group into pairs and give each pair a piece of one foot long rope. Instruct each group of two that they each must hold onto one end of the rope for the entire activity (as though they were handcuffed together), or you may actually tie (or tape) their wrists together.

Once the partners are attached to each other by the rope, give them various tasks. Create different task depending on the equipment that is available. Some suggested tasks are:
1. Go through an obstacle course
2. Run a given distance
3. Shoot and make five baskets

4. Play partners ping pong against another set of partners
5. Do exercises (jumping jacks, sit ups, push ups, etc.)

If anyone lets go of the rope at anytime, they must start over or lose all of their points for that game. For added incentive, allow each team to do any timed activities twice, timing it each time so that they may try to improve their own time.

Discussion Prompts

1. Did having a partner make life easier or more difficult for you? Why?
2. What did you do to help or hinder your partner? Why?
3. When in life is it better to have a partner helping you?
4. Who do you have in your life that you feel hinders you? Why?
5. Who do you have in your life that is a helpful partner? What does s/he do to help you?

Variations

- If the use of the term "jailbreak" seems inappropriate for your group explain that they are "Siamese" twins instead of "handcuffed together".
- Tie their ankles together in addition to, or instead of, their wrists.

THREE HIT VOLLEYBALL

When playing a competitive game it is easy to focus on the score and on who is winning. But, when the use of teamwork gains points for your team (as it does in this game) the focus changes from winning to teamwork.

Objective
To increase the amount of teamwork used in an average volleyball game.

Who
People who have difficulty using teamwork when playing a competitive game.

Group Size
6 to 12 is ideal

Materials
- Volleyball
- Volleyball net

Description
Play a regular game of volleyball by the normal rules but add the following rule to the game. Whenever a team hits the ball three times on its side before returning it over the net, that team is awarded an extra point. The extra points should be counted by the teams playing and simply added to the score each time there is a serve. A team may earn extra points at anytime, even when they aren't in possession of the serve.

This may sound like a game that can get confusing and that it may be difficult to keep track of the score, but if the people in your group are anything like the people in the groups that I play with, these extra points are often challenging and hard to come by.

Discussion Prompts

1. Was there more or less teamwork used on your team as a result of the new rule?
2. Is this game more or less fun when you are focused on teamwork?
3. Are sports more fun for you to play when teamwork is involved or not?
4. What do you do when on a team to increase teamwork?
5. In your life can you think of anything you can do to help others by using your teamwork skills?

Variation

➲ Use a beach ball or lighter weight ball to start with and then switch to a regular volleyball when the group seems ready for more of a challenge.

PAPER TOWER

It seems that most everyone likes a good challenge. This is why there are so many competitive games, extreme sports and contests to be won in our world. Sometimes we meet the challenge and find that it isn't enough: we aren't satisfied. We want to go higher, be better or move onto something bigger.

Challenges are for individuals as well as for groups. This activity is one challenge that is easy but hard at the same time. Everyone can be involved in the activity and people don't seem to want to quit. Each team wants to keep building the tower taller and higher than they had built it before even if it means starting over many times. The challenge in this game is what brings people together to work as a team.

Objective
To work as a part of a team and to problem solve as a team. To continue an activity even if frustration occurs.

Who
People who need to learn to work as a part of a team or group in a situation where it is possible to isolate oneself and work alone.

Group Size
2 to 10 participants

Materials
➲ A stack of 8x11 pieces of paper (copy machine kind is the best)
~ This is a great time to use up old scrap paper that is lying around!! ~

Description
Simply give the group a stack of paper and nothing else. Instruct the group that they must build the tallest tower that they possibly can, using only the paper given to them. No tape, gum, paper clips, etc.

allowed. (Sometimes I limit the group to fifteen sheets of paper; other times I give them whatever I can round up.)

There are many different ways this activity can be done, but I find people work even harder at it if I give them a goal (i.e. "I've seen a tower five sheets high (the long ways) before"). When I say this, everyone wants to get at least five and hopefully more. The goal must be challenging but also realistic for the group to reach. Or have more than one group attempting to get the tallest tower.

Hint: There are many ways to build a paper tower but one of the better ways is to fold each piece into three sections then open up the paper slightly and stack them on top of each other or place a horizontal sheet between each stacked paper.

Discussion Prompts

1. What steps did the group take in order to solve this problem?
2. Did everyone contribute? If so, how? If not, why?
3. Did anyone in the group get frustrated at any point? If so, how was it handled?
4. What things did the group do to show teamwork?
5. As a member of the team what role did you take on in this activity?
6. When in your life is it important to use teamwork?

RADIO BROADCAST

You can hear just about anything on the radio these days - news, weather, sports, advice, and of course any kind of music that there is. The radio is almost always live, sometimes it's funny, sometimes informing and usually entertaining. A simple broadcast takes a team of people to create, and teamwork is always an essential element needed to pull off a great show.

Objective
To show teamwork by working together as a group to create a radio broadcast. To promote group bonding by sharing what it is that people know and observe about each other.

Who
People who could benefit from working with others when making group decisions and who need to improve on their social skills.

Group Size
4 or more

Materials
- Paper
- Pens or pencils

Description
Divide the group into at least two smaller groups with two to six people on each team. Give each group a list of the names of the people on one of the other teams and instruct them that they must create a radio broadcast about that group and give them the following specific instructions.

As a group you have twenty minutes to create a radio broadcast about the events and activities that have occurred over the past couple of days (or whatever time frame you choose to use). *You may include poems, sound effects, songs, weather, a sports cast etc. You <u>must</u> include an update about each person from the other group who is on the list you were given.*

(Sometimes you may want to add a note about the presentation being appropriate if you think the group could use the reminder.)

Give each group a place to work that is separate from the others so they can work without being heard.

After the twenty minutes bring the groups back together and ask them to present their radio broadcast. You may allow one person to present the entire thing or for added teamwork, ownership and participation require each person to take part in some aspect of the broadcast that they have helped to create.

Discussion Prompts

1. Was everyone included in creating your broadcast? If so, why? If not, why?
2. How did each person contribute to the final product?
3. How does it feel to be a part of a team that creates something that everyone is proud of?
4. Do you have a group or team in your life that you feel proud to belong to? Why?
5. Have you ever been a part of a group that was doing things that you weren't proud of? What did you do and why?
6. What can you do if you find yourself on a team or in a group that you don't want to be part of anymore because you don't agree with what they are doing?

DiNNER FOR TWO

Pooling your resources together for the good of the group isn't always a very easy thing to do. The men and women of congress each come from different states and want many different things. Only when they get together and decide what's important for the country does anything happen (and each single state may not always get what they want). This activity is about pooling your resources, thinking of others and making decisions for the good of the group rather than for the good of the individual.

Objective
For a group of people to work together to problem solve, make decisions and be considerate of others (or the group may suffer the consequences).

Who
People who need to learn to think of what is best for a group of people rather than being focused on their own needs and desires.

Group Size
4 or more

Materials
- ⊃ $2 for each group member
- ⊃   Transportation to the local grocery store

Description
This activity is for any group that eats a meal together, or plan a time when this can be done. Instead of following the usual routine for a meal, give each person in the group $2 and take them to the local grocery store. Instruct the group that whatever they buy will be what the group eats for dinner. Each person may chose to get their own

thing, but they will soon find out that $2 doesn't go very far and will remember that everyone must share what they have bought.

Hopefully the group will get together and plan a meal and pool their money together or divvy up the items for a meal (i.e. one person buys spaghetti, others buy sauce, bread, drinks, salad veggies, salad dressing and dessert to form a complete meal). If the group doesn't do it this way and everyone gets their own thing or junk food that's OK; it makes for a fun and interesting object lesson.

Discussion Prompts

1. How do you feel about the meal that the group created?
2. What process did the group go through to create this meal?
3. What is the most difficult part of making group decisions for you? Why?
4. When do you have to make decisions with others?
5. What are some things to remember when making decisions with others?

SNEAK A PEEK

Communication is a key element when working with others on a group project. This is especially true on a construction project. The architect draws up the plans which the foreman must interpret, understand, and communicate to his/her workers so they know what they must do to complete the building. This activity is a small version of a construction site, and just as much communication and teamwork are needed from all those involved.

Objective
To work as a team to complete a difficult task.

Who
People who could benefit from working together with others in order to learn social skills. People who need practice listening to and following directions that are given to them.

Group Size
4 or more

Materials
➲ Building blocks or something similar (i.e. Lego's®, Popsicle® sticks, etc.)

Description
Build a small sculpture, or design with some of the building material (make it easy for lower functioning groups and more complex for higher functioning groups) and hide it from the group. Divide the group into small teams of two to five members each. Give each team enough building material so that they could duplicate what you have already created.

Place the original sculpture in a place that is hidden but equal distance to all the groups. Ask one group member from each team to come at the same time to look at the sculpture for five seconds in order to try to memorize it as much as possible before returning to his/her respective teams.

After they run back to their teams, they have twenty-five seconds to instruct their teams how to build the structure so that it looks like the one that has been hidden. After the twenty-five seconds, ask each team to send up another member of their group who gets a chance to "sneak a peek" before returning to their individual teams. Continue in this pattern until one of the teams successfully duplicates the original sculpture.

Build a different sculpture for any additional rounds of this game.

Discussion Prompts
1. What parts of this activity involved teamwork?
2. What did each person do in your group to help?
3. Why is teamwork important when working with a group?
4. What are some important elements of teamwork?
5. How can being good at teamwork help you in your daily life?

Variation
➲ Give each team a pad of paper and a pen or pencil to take notes on for their five second observation.

LIGHTHOUSE

A lighthouse guides the way for ships in the fog and dark of night and away from dangers. The captain of a ship must have full confidence in each and every lighthouse if s/he is to get the ship to its destination on time and safely.

In this activity the trust between the "captain" of the ship and a "lighthouse" is the key to the ship delivering it's "cargo" on time and the key to building trust among group members.

Objective

For each person to take on different roles in a single teamwork activity in order to support his/her team.

Who

People who need to learn to work with others, trust them and rely on them for help. People who need to learn to be trustworthy.

Group Size

4 or more

Materials

- ➲ Various obstacles
- ➲ Blindfolds
- ➲ Pieces of wrapped candy

Description

Blindfold one person and put him/her at one end of a room or outdoor area that has various obstacles in it (i.e. rocks, cones, chairs, trees, etc.). Select at least three of the remaining group members to be "lighthouses" and ask them to stand in various places along the obstacle course.

Give the blindfolded person a handful of candy (one piece for each *lighthouse*). The job of each *lighthouse* is to guide the *cargo ship* (blindfolded person) through the rough waters (obstacle course) safely so that the *cargo* (candy) can be delivered to each *lighthouse*.

The first *lighthouse* must verbally guide the *cargo ship* through the obstacles and directly to the *lighthouse*, if this is done successfully the *ship* will deliver one piece of candy to that person.

The only *lighthouse* allowed to give directions at a given time is the one that the *ship* is headed for, but he/she may give support and encouragement after the person has gone past him/her. Any *lighthouse* whose area the *ship* has not come to yet must remain quiet until the *ship* reaches his/her area.

If the *ship* is put into danger by crashing into an obstacle the guiding *lighthouse* does not get any candy. Or, if the *lighthouse* is unable to guide the person successfully to him/her and the ship passes on by then this person receives no candy and the next *lighthouse* takes over.

Allow the group members to take turns in the different positions, and for large groups you may have more than one obstacle course going at once.

Discussion Prompts

1. Did you feel safe when you were the "cargo ship"? Why or why not?
2. Do you think people in this group would have kept you as safe if candy wasn't involved? Why?
3. Do you have people in your life that you trust to guide you? Who and why?
4. Do you have people in your life that give you support when you need it? If so, who and what do they do? If not, why do you think this is and where can you go to find support when you need it?
5. How do you feel about the group as a result of this activity?

Variation

⮑ Put moving objects or people into the area the ship will be moving through to act as "floating logs". These objects or people should move through the area quietly while the lighthouses try to steer the ship around them.

SELF-ESTEEM

Memories are made up of experiences, fun times, bad times, and most importantly the things that others have said to us in our lifetime. People who have a memory filled with positive experiences and good times and who have heard an abundance of positive comments from others are more likely to have a healthy self-esteem than someone who has heard numerous negative comments and whose life has been filled with bad memories.

People have such a strong inner need to be recognized, validated, and seen as important that when praise is given, it is treasured and remembered for a long time. When a child leaves the hospital where I work and then returns later, it is not uncommon for him/her to tell me that s/he kept a certain self-esteem activity, especially if it was a page of positive compliments given to this child from his/her peers. This is evidence of our need to hang onto the positive feedback given to us from others. Just as important is a trophy collection, special letter from a friend or even a simple hug and smile.

Unfortunately one negative comment or experience seems to stay with a person longer and is felt more deeply than a wonderful experience. People who have a low self-esteem often have numerous bad memories in their past, and it may take many positive experiences to undo the damage.

Another unfortunate fact of life is that as we grow older we lose the innocence of our childhood and with it we lose the freedom to give ourselves the positive comments we need when the compliments are lacking from others. Young children are able to build their own self-esteem by clapping when they do something good and telling others about their achievements with a big toothy grin. Society doesn't allow adults and adolescents to praise themselves without being seen as conceited and stuck-up, so we must rely on the praise of others.

Since society has set the rules, people must find other ways to build positive self-esteem in themselves and in each other, and this is where games come in. Games allow people to give more compliments than they would normally and to hear much needed words of praise. A number of self-esteem activities have the same goals, objectives and hopeful outcomes, but in order to undo the damage that has been done after many years of building up a low self-esteem, people need to hear positive things over and over, and too much is never enough.

SELF-ESTEEM GAMES AND ACTIVITIES

LOVE LINE

If we take the time to observe those around us more closely, we will notice many positive and wonderful things about each person that we may have not noticed before. When people take time to give and receive compliments the self-esteem of all those involved is affected in a very positive way. This activity gives people time to reflect on the qualities of the others in the group and to pass these thoughts along.

Objective
To communicate feelings and to improve the self-esteem of others.

Who
People who have low self-esteem.
Group members should be familiar with each other.

Group Size
4 or more

Materials
- ➲ 1 large envelope for each person
- ➲ A stack of 3x5 cards
- ➲ Pens or pencils
- ➲ A piece of heavy string or rope (length depends on group size)

Description
This activity can go on for a short period of time or it can continue over a long period of time.

Each person in the group puts his/her name on an envelope, punches a hole in the corner and threads it through the string. Attach the rope or heavy duty string (that is threaded with the envelopes) along a wall or between two chairs so that the middle section with all of the envelopes on it is hanging free.

Provide a stack of 3x5 cards and pens or pencils for the group members to use at any time. Inform everyone that whenever they have free time they may use the cards to write a nice note or comment to anyone else in the group on one of the cards and then put the note into that person's envelope.

Encourage the group to write positive notes to as many people as they can. At a designated time allow everyone to read their "love line" notes. Or whenever a group member leaves the group s/he may take his/her envelope and read the notes in it as a way to leave the group on a positive note.

Discussion Prompts
1. How do you feel after reading all of the notes that you have been given?
2. How did you feel when writing nice notes to other people?
3. Why is it important to be able to accept and to give compliments?

Variation
➲ Ask each person to write one note for everyone in the group.

GLORY STORY

As you begin to read a story, the author introduces each character by giving detailed descriptions, until finally the character becomes clear and vivid in your mind. By the end of the story each character has a distinct personality with unique traits, strengths, weaknesses and talents.

The stories that will be created in this activity build on the strengths and characteristics of each special individual in the group.

Objective

To increase self-esteem by recognizing positive traits in others and by hearing positive things about ourselves.

Who

People who have the ability to be creative and who could benefit from hearing positive things about themselves.
Participants should be familiar with each other.

Group Size

2 or more

Materials

➲ Paper
➲ Pens or pencils

Description

Divide the group into small groups of one to six participants each. Separate the groups so that they cannot hear each other. Supply each group with a couple of sheets of paper and a pen or pencil. Assign each group to one of the other groups and ask them to write down all of the names of the people from that other group on their paper.

Ask each group to write a story that includes all of the members of the other group as the characters, with each character in the story using his/her positive traits, strong points and assets as a part of the story line. Once all of the stories are written ask each group to read their story to the entire group.

Discussion Prompts

1. Were you surprised by any of the attributes that the other group gave to your character?
2. Can you think of any more positive traits that you could add to your character or to anyone else's character in the group?
3. How can you use your strong points to improve the life that you live and to make your own "character" into what you really want for yourself?

Variation

➲ Have each person write a story about themselves and add other members of their families, friends, or group members as the other characters.

CAMPAIGN CRAZE

When politicians run a campaign they sell themselves by telling everyone about all their successes, strong points, values and positive traits. Creating your own campaign takes guts, and it isn't easy to stand up in front of a bunch of people and brag about yourself; but it can be fun if you get creative, a bit outrageous, and most of all a bit bold.

Objective
For people to recognize and to verbalize positive traits that they possess.

Who
People who have difficulty recognizing their own positive attributes.

Group Size
2 or more

Materials
- ➔ Paper
- ➔ Pens or pencils
- ➔ Colored markers
- ➔ Tape
- ➔ Scissors
- ➔ Optional: paints, glitter, ribbons, glue, etc.

Description
Inform everyone that they each will be running for an office of their choice. Each person will need to run an extensive campaign in their attempt to become elected (it's all pretend of course). Each person must then create the following campaign items: a poster, campaign button/s, an original speech, a slogan and anything else they can think of (some people even write their own song). Encourage everyone to base their campaign on all of their positive attributes and traits.

Once everyone is finished, ask each person to present his/her campaign to the rest of the group. After each presentation there is usually a round of applause from the rest of the group. During the campaign encourage people to put their posters up on the wall and to wear their buttons (they may even wish to hand out buttons for others to wear).

Discussion Prompts

1. How did you feel when you were presenting your campaign?
2. Was it difficult or easy for you to think of positive things about yourself for the campaign?
3. Would you ever consider running for a school or political office? Why or why not?
4. What did you learn about others in the group when doing this activity?

BODY BEAUTIFUL

Our bodies are made up of many different parts and each part contributes to making us special. Some of us have strong legs and can run fast, while others have talented fingers to create beautiful art. Each person contributes to the world with his/her own special talents and unique abilities.

Objective
For people to identify positive traits that they possess and to verbally share them with the rest of the group.

Who
People who have a poor self-image.

Group Size
1 or more

Materials
- ➲ A large roll of butcher paper or newsprint
- ➲ Colored markers
- ➲ Scissors

Description
Give each person a piece of the paper that is large enough for them to lie down on so that someone else can trace their body. Once each person has been traced, ask each person to write in each of their body parts all of the positive things that they can do with that part of their body (i.e. on an arm someone might write "gives hugs", on the mouth write "good singer", on an ear "good listener" etc.). Allow time at the end for each person to share their creation with the group.

Discussion Prompts

1. Did you think of positive traits about yourself that you hadn't recognized before?
2. Were you surprised by how many things you thought of (or didn't think of)?
3. Is it hard for you to say nice things about yourself? Why?

Variation

➲ Write positive things on each other's body outlines.

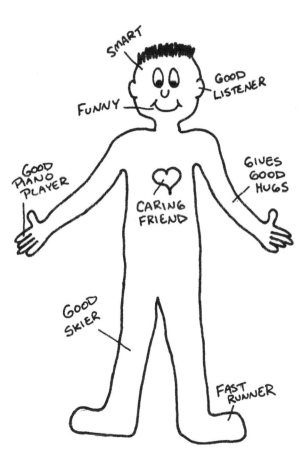

BOLD BiLLBOARD

Billboards are big, eye catching, and colorful. They are made to be seen and looked at and to give a message. Some people are like billboards because they want others to notice them. Others are shy and reserved without getting much attention. In this activity those who are shy can become the center of attention by creating a bold billboard for all to see.

Objective
To give people the opportunity to express their positive traits and attributes in a non-threatening manner.

Who
People with a low self-esteem who have difficulty expressing their own unique, positive traits.

Group Size
1 or more

Materials
- ⮑ One large sheet of paper (i.e. butcher paper, newsprint) for each person
- ⮑ Tempera paints, paint brushes and/or fat colored markers
- ⮑ Tape

Description
Give each person a large piece of paper, paint and/or markers. Instruct the group members that they must create a billboard that is big, bold, and colorful. More important than the colors are the words and pictures that reflect the positive traits of the person creating it. Each person must advertise him/herself through a billboard by highlighting his/her own unique positive traits.

Once everyone has completed their billboard, ask each person to read their billboard to the group and then hang it up on the wall if there is room to do so.

Discussion Prompts

1. Did anyone have any difficulty thinking of things to put on your billboard? If so, why?
2. How did you feel when others were looking at your billboard?
3. Why is it important to be able to identify positive things about yourself? Why is it important to be able to tell other people these things?

MARVELOUS MOBILES

Mobiles are fun pieces of art that are often created by kids at camp. With a new twist on an old theme, a mobile can be changed from a classic art project to a new self-esteem builder.

Objective
For people to recognize things that they do well and to be able to verbalize these things to others in the group.

Who
People who have a poor self-image and who have difficulty recognizing things that they do well.

Group Size
1 or more

Materials
- Sticks (about 2 feet in length)
- Yarn
- Construction paper
- Colored markers
- Scissors

Description
Give each person one of the sticks, or you may choose to have the group go for a walk in order to collect their own sticks. Lay out all of the supplies for the group to use and ask them to use the paper and pens to make pictures or symbols of the things that they do well. When they are finished creating their pictures, have them cut pieces of string in different lengths (about one to two feet long) that they can use to tie their pictures to the stick, so that the pictures are hanging on the string.

Once each person has created his/her "marvelous mobile", allow time for everyone to share what they have created with the rest of the group. If the group meets regularly in a room, you may have them hang up their mobiles for all to see.

Discussion Prompts
1. How does it make you feel to know that you are really good at something?
2. How do you feel when you tell others the things that you are good at doing?
3. How can telling others help you to recognize the things that you do well?
4. Are there situations in your life when it's OK to say good things about yourself?

Variation
➲ Cut pictures from magazines of things that represent what each person does well, glue them to paper that is cut out, and hang these pictures from the string.

POSITIVE PRIDE

Pictures are hung on the refrigerator door for all to see because when someone makes something that they are proud of they want to share it with others. This makes them feel special. This activity is about making something special and being proud of the end result.

Objective
For people to feel pride when putting time and effort into making something and to gain self-esteem from doing so.

Who
People who have difficulty finding positive aspects of their own lives.

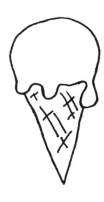

Group Size
1 to 10 participants

Materials
- Ice-cream Maker
- Ingredients needed for making home made ice cream

Description
Provide the group with an ice cream maker, instructions and the ingredients needed for making homemade ice cream. Allow the group to make the ice cream without any assistance from any of the leaders.

Once the ice-cream is finished the group can enjoy the wonderful treat while having a discussion about how it feels to work hard to make something that they can be proud of in the end.

Discussion Prompts

1. How do you feel about the ice cream that you have made?
2. How do you feel after accomplishing a task that takes time and effort?
3. Do you do anything in your life that you are proud of doing?
4. How can you find activities that will help to improve your self-esteem?

Variation

➲ Any project that requires time and effort may be used for this activity.

SAME LETTER, DIFFERENT NAME

Ambitious, athletic, artistic and altruistic, - there are plenty more words that begin with "A" that create a positive description of people we know or even of ourselves. Thinking of new words from A to Z that are descriptive of the people we know is the purpose of this game, and with added competition it's lots of fun. The best part, though, is getting to hear positive descriptive words about yourself at the end of this fast paced thinking game.

Objective
For group members to recognize the positive traits that exist in each other.

Who
People who could benefit from hearing positive comments about themselves. Group members should be familiar with each other.

Group Size
4 to 20 participants

Materials
- ➲ Paper
- ➲ Pens or pencils
- ➲ A timer or stopwatch
- ➲ An envelope filled with the letters of the alphabet (written on small slips of paper)

Description
Divide the group into two even teams and ask each team to write down on one piece of paper all the names of the people on their team

and on the other team. Once all the names are written down, select a letter of the alphabet from the envelope. Inform the teams what letter was chosen and give them two minutes to work as a team to think of a positive word, or words beginning with the chosen letter that describes each person. For example, if the letter H was chosen and the names John, Amy, and Craig were on the list my team may come up with:

John - **H**ard worker
Amy - **H**onest, **H**umble
Craig - **H**andsome

Once the time limit is up bring the two teams together and ask them to each read their list to the group. For added fun and competition you may give each team a point for every word on their list that isn't on the other team's list.

Play as many rounds of this game as you have time for. You may want to make specific rules for the activity (i.e. you must think of at least one word for each person on the list). The discussion may be held at the end of the game or hold a short discussion after each round.

Discussion Prompts

1. How do you feel about the words that were chosen to describe you?
2. Were you surprised by any of the words used to describe you? If so why?
3. Did anyone give any ideas for the a word that you would use to describe yourself?
4. Is it easy or hard to think of positive words to describe others? Yourself? Why?

Variations

- ➲ Don't give a time limit; instead give bonus points to the team that thinks of a word to describe everyone on the list first.
- ➲ With a large group don't include your own team on your list, instead just think of words to describe the members of the other team, or break the group up into more than two teams.

TRUE TALENTS

If we gain our self-esteem from being the best we can be, then a high self-esteem would be easy to come by. Unfortunately in today's world we compare ourselves to others; and if we don't measure up, we become failures in our own mind. This activity is about winning, losing, and trying to be better than others. In the end the winners are those who succeed in being the best they can be.

Objective

For individual's to recognize that everyone has different talents and gifts, and that each person is unique and special. To help people to understand that it is OK to not win a talent contest or to get the best grades because as long as they try their best and know that they have their own special talents, then they will be able to have a positive self-esteem.

Who

People who base their self-esteem on how much they succeed and who get down on themselves when they lose or who feel they never do good enough.

Group Size

3 or more

Materials

- ⇒ Bubble Gum
- ⇒ Various supplies

Description

Start the group by giving everyone a piece of gum and have a bubble-gum blowing contest. After you determine who the winner is, write his/her name up on a chalkboard or other place for all to see. After the bubble-blowing contest move on to other talent contests.

An idea of a contest to use for this game is a drawing contest where you allow everyone in the group to cast three votes to determine who the winner is.

Another talent contest idea is to give everyone a jump rope and see who can jump rope the longest without making a mistake.

Then in a gym or outside area where there is a basketball hoop allow everyone to get ten tries to make as many baskets as s/he can.

The name of the winner of each contest is put up on the board. I then ask everyone to think about what talent contest they would do really well in. For some it may be a "best listener" contest, for others it may be "the best big sister", "best soccer player", etc. Ask each person to put his/her name on the board along with the type of contest in which s/he would succeed. Focus the discussion on how each person is different and unique.

Discussion Prompts

Prior to the discussion questions ask the group to notice how there are different winners for different activities and to think about why this is. Focus discussion on how individuals are unique and how each person in the group is good at different things and that this is what makes everyone special and unique.

1. What type of talent contest would you win? (This could be anything from a big sister contest to best listener or great golfer, singer, etc.)
2. Do you ever base your self worth on being better than others or on not feeling like you are as good as others?
3. Why is it important for you to recognize your own unique, positive traits?

KiNG'S THRONE

When a king sits on his throne, people bring him gifts, honor him with compliments, and add to the power he already has. To be king for a day or even just for a little while would be wonderful. In this activity people get to be kings and can gain the power of a good self-esteem by hearing compliments from others as they sit on their thrones.

Objective
To increase self-esteem by receiving positive comments from others.

Who
People with a low self-esteem that have difficulty accepting compliments from others.

Group Size
4 to 10 participants

Materials
- Paper
- Pens or pencils
- Chair

Description
Give each person a piece of paper and a pen or pencil. Each person must write down a positive comment about each member of the group. Once everyone has completed writing down their compliments, select one member of the group to sit in a chair (the King's Throne) that is placed so everyone else can see this person. Each person then takes a turn and reads the positive comment that they have written to the person in the "throne" who is "king".

Allow enough time for each person to take a turn sitting on the throne and for everyone to read their comments to each other.

Discussion Prompts

1. How did you feel when you were on the King's Throne?
2. How does it make you feel when you hear positive comments about yourself?
3. Why is it important to hear positive things from others?
4. Do you more often hear positive comments made about yourself or negative comments?
5. If you mainly hear negative comments, how can you put yourself in a situation where you will hear more positive comments?

Variation

➲ Inform the group ahead of time about the activity so they have more time to prepare their compliments.

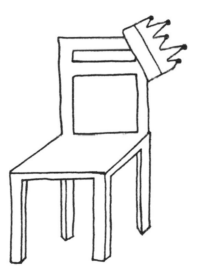

THE COST OF SARCASM

Some people have the gift of being very funny through their sarcastic sense of humor and usually have everyone around them in constant laughter. Sarcastic humor can be very funny, but it can also be very hurtful if said at the wrong time, in a negative manner, or if it is said about someone else.

This game helps to open people's eyes to the amount of negative or sarcastic comments said and how these comments can be hurtful to others.

This game has also been a wonderful anger management activity for individuals who have trouble controlling their anger, but who can show the ability to maintain complete composure when a prize is involved.

Objective
To understand how sarcastic and negative comments affect others and to realize how often we make negative comments without even realizing that others may be hurt or offended by what was said.

Who
People who frequently make sarcastic or negative comments.
People who are easily hurt by what others say.

Group Size
3 to 10 participants

Materials
➲ A wide variety of board games or card games
➲ Play money

Description
Prior to the game give each person a set amount of the play money, depending on the value of your play money, (for example give each

person five $100 dollar bills). Inform the group that the object of the game is to be the person with the most money in the end.

There are a variety of ways that people can gain or lose money. Money can be given or taken away by the group leader for good or bad sportsmanship. Money can be gained for winning a particular game. Or most importantly money can be taken away from anyone who makes negative or sarcastic comments (even the slightest roll of the eyes can be worthy of a $100 penalty) during the course of a game. Whenever anyone makes such a comment the first person who calls out that person's name can take $100 dollars away from him/her and then keep it. The leader should judge if the comment was worthy of a penalty.

Once you establish the rules of the game, set up a variety of board games, card games or any other interactive game for the group to play. For added fun or effect, have a prize for the person with the most money at the end of the game.

Discussion Prompts

1. Did people make negative comments during this game or was everyone able to be polite? Why or why not?
2. Were you surprised by the amount of negative or sarcastic comments that were made during the game?
3. Why do you think people make negative or sarcastic comments?
4. How do these type of comments affect you?
5. How do these comments relate to your self-esteem?

GOOD GRAFFITI

Graffiti is a way of letting people know you have been somewhere, that you exist, a way of leaving your mark. It used to be "Billy Bob loves Peggy Sue" with a big heart or "Joey was here". Now graffiti has turned into a territory marker for gangs and a way to rebel for "taggers". In this activity graffiti is used to help build self-esteem in a fun way.

Objective
For people to express their positive qualities in a non-threatening manner and to give compliments to others.

Who
People who have difficulty recognizing and expressing to others what their unique qualities are. People who could benefit from hearing positive comments from others.

Group Size
3 or more

Materials
- ⮑ A large roll of paper
- ⮑ Scissors
- ⮑ Tempera paint and paint brushes
- ⮑ Masking tape

Description
Cut a large sheet of paper for each person in the group and lay it out on the floor or tape each piece up on a blank wall. Provide the group with paint and paint brushes. Instruct the group members to make "graffiti" on their paper. First, everyone should put their names on their papers and then paint two positive words describing themselves. Then

each person must go around the room and paint at least one nice word or comment on everyone else's paper (you may need to add a rule about no "gang writing" or gang symbols, if appropriate for your group).

Once everyone is finished, allow time for them to read their own papers before moving on to discussion. If there is a large wall to hang the posters on, you may wish to do this as a group and encourage teamwork when doing so.

Discussion Prompts

1. Were you surprised by what anyone else wrote?
2. How do you feel after reading your graffiti?
3. Was it easier to think of nice things about yourself or others? Why?
4. Was it easier to make comments on the paper than it is to say them? Why?
5. Has anyone in this group ever painted graffiti? Why? Is this a good thing for you to do?

Variations

➲ This may be done with colored markers and smaller sheets of paper.
➲ If a large outside blank wall is available you may use sidewalk chalk to write "good graffiti" on the wall.
➲ Allow people to just write on their own paper and to create "graffiti" that is a positive description of themselves.

STOREFRONT

On a movie set there are many storefront props used to create a city, and in the windows of these pretend stores there are a variety of items that are typical of the things one would find in that kind of shop. Each store adds its own unique personality to the street scene that is being created - just as each individual person adds uniqueness and special qualities to a group.

Objective
For people to recognize what is valuable and unique about themselves and to be a able to share these attributes with others.

Who
People who have a difficult time identifying their own positive qualities. People with a low self-esteem.

Group Size
1 or more

Materials
- ➔ A large roll of paper
- ➔ Scissors
- ➔ Tempera Paints, paint brushes
- ➔ Fat tipped colored markers

Description
Provide each person in the group with a large sheet of paper, paints and colored markers. Instruct the group that they are going to make a "movie set" and that the scene they are creating is a city street. A variety of storefronts will be needed for the set. Ask each person to create a unique storefront with items, posters, signs, colors etc. that represents who they are (i.e. a person might have books in his/her store

for love of reading, a pair of skis for someone who is a ski instructor, and a tape recorder for a person who is a good listener). For this activity it is sometimes best to have a sample already made to help give people the idea.

After everyone has finished with their storefront, hang these store "windows" on a wall or place them somewhere for all to see and allow each person to explain their store to everyone else in the group.

Discussion Prompts

1. What did you learn about yourself as a result of this activity?
2. What did you learn about others as a result of this activity?
3. Do you usually display all of your positive attributes or do you hide them away in the "back storage closet"? Why?
4. Why is it important to recognize your own positive qualities?
5. How does your "store" contribute to its city?

PERSONALIZED PLATES

When traveling, it is always fun to look at the different license plates from different states. Each one is unique and different so that it can stand out from the others as it represents its home state. Just as license plates are different so are people. Creating your own license plate can set you apart from others as unique and special.

Objective
For people to recognize their own individual unique traits and to be able to share these with others.

Who
People who have difficulty recognizing their own individual, unique traits.

Group Size
1 or more

Materials
- ➲ Paper
- ➲ Pens or pencils
- ➲ Colored markers, crayons or paint
- ➲ Optional: glitter, glue, colored paper, scissors, etc.

Description
Start the activity by asking the group to think of local state license plates and to describe what is on them and why it looks like it does. For example the state of Washington has Mt. Rainier on it's license plate because this is a predominant landmark in the state and even a national park. Arizona has a cacti on it's plates to represent the desert that is found in that state.

Ask group members to think about what their own license plate would look like and why. What colors would be on it, what year would the tabs be, what pictures would it have on it, what would your state be called? What would your personalized plate say with its letters and numbers, and would it have a state slogan or not? Then give the group the opportunity to create their own original plates with the materials provided.

After everyone has completed their own personalized plates, allow time for everyone to share with the group what they have created and ask them to explain the meaning of everything on their plates.

Discussion Prompts

1. Was it easy or hard for you to create your own personalized plate?
2. Why is it hard to recognize the things that make us unique from other people?
3. Why is it important to find your own unique qualities?
4. What did you learn about the others in the group that you didn't know before?

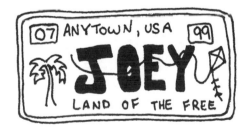

TO YOU, BUT FROM WHO?

Sometimes it is difficult to hear and accept compliments, especially when the compliment is given in front of other people. But if those compliments are a part of a guessing game, they are easier to hear and even more fun to give.

Objective

For people to give and receive many positive comments as a way of improving their self-esteem.

Who

People with a low self-esteem who could benefit from hearing positive comments about themselves as well as those who need practice giving positive comments to others.

Group Size

4 to 15 participants

Materials

- ⊃ One envelope per person
- ⊃ Paper
- ⊃ Pens or pencils

Description

Give each person an envelope, pen or pencil and several small slips of paper. Ask everyone to put their names on the envelopes and then pass their envelope to the person sitting next to them.

Once you receive your neighbor's envelope you write down an attribute that you admire about that person on a slip of paper. Add your name and then place the paper in the envelope. Continue passing the envelopes around until everyone has written down a comment for everyone else in the group.

Once all of the envelopes are full, they should be passed to the leader. The leader then selects one of the envelopes and selects a comment to read out loud to that person, without reading the name of the person who wrote it. The person whom the comment was written about will then try to guess who wrote the comment, and if s/he guesses correctly, s/he receives a point. The object is to be the one in the end with the most points. Go around the circle reading one comment from each envelope before starting over with the first person. Continue in this manner until all the comments are read from each person's envelope. After the game is finished, each person may collect their own envelope and keep it as a reminder of all their good qualities.

Discussion Prompts

1. How do you feel after hearing all those positive things about yourself?
2. Do you often hear positive things from others? How does this affect you?
3. Will you keep this envelope? Why or why not?
4. Why is it important to hear positive things from others?
5. Do you believe everything that was said about you? Why or why not?

Variation

➲ After everyone has written attributes down and filled the envelopes, redistribute the envelopes among the group members, so that each person takes turns reading a comment from the envelope that they have. This is simply a way to get everyone more involved in the process.

ME ON THE TV

Do we believe everything we hear and see? The people who create TV commercials hope that we do and try to sell us their products based upon our willingness to buy into their ideas. Each commercial must convince us of the positive aspects of what they are trying to sell. For this activity the product is each person in the group, and each individual has the job of trying to sell him/herself to all those who are watching.

Objective
To identify and advertise one's positive traits.

Who
People who could benefit from naming their own positive traits and who need to develop the ability to tell others what these traits are.

Group Size
4 or more

Materials
➲ Paper
➲ Pens or pencils

Description
Supply each person in the group with a piece of paper and a pen or pencil. Instruct the group that each person must create a TV commercial that advertises his/her positive traits. Each commercial must contain at least 3 traits and must try to convince the audience that the person being advertised has special gifts, talents, or personality traits that make this person outstanding! Allow time for each person to use the piece of paper to create a screenplay for his/her commercial. Each person must be in his/her own commercial and may use as many of the other group members as needed to play characters or to be props

as needed. You should set a time limit for planning and for how long each commercial can be based upon how many participants there are.

Discussion Prompts
1. Was this a difficult thing for you to do? Why or why not?
2. Would it have been easier to make a commercial for your friend than for yourself? Why?
3. What did your learn about others in the group when doing this activity?
4. Why is it so hard to tell others the good things about yourself?

Variations
⊃ If a video camera is available, tape the commercials and view them later as a group.
⊃ If the group meets regularly, give this as an assignment and have them bring their screenplays to the next group, ready to go.
⊃ Have group members write commercials about each other.

BALLOON BUST

Receiving compliments from others is one of the best ways to build a good self-esteem, but more than just hearing compliments is important. You must be able to accept these compliments and believe them to be true.

Objective
To give and receive compliments. To be able to accept these compliments to be true and for people to recognize their own positive qualities.

Who
People who have a low self-esteem who could benefit from receiving compliments. People who have difficulty saying nice things to others and who need the practice. Group members should be familiar with each other.

Group Size
4 or more

Materials
- 1 large balloon (not inflated) per person
- Permanent markers
- Paper
- Pens or pencils
- Scissors

Description
Pass out the balloons so that each person has one and ask everyone to blow up their balloon but not to tie them and then to write their names on their own balloons with the permanent markers. Once everyone has their names on their own balloons, ask them to let the air out.

Now pass out the paper, scissors and pens or pencils to each person. Gather the group into a circle and instruct the group members to pass their balloons to the person sitting next to them. Once everyone has somebody else's balloon, each person needs to cut a piece of paper small enough so that s/he can write a positive comment or compliment on it and then put it in the balloon (it is a good idea to put the name of the person the compliment is for on each piece of paper in case they scatter later). The comments should reflect the person whose name is on the balloon and be complimentary. Continue to pass the balloons around the room so everyone gets the opportunity to give a compliment to everyone else in the group.

Once this process is completed, ask everyone to hand the balloon they have back to the person whose name is on it. Ask the group if they want to know what the compliments are that are written on the paper inside their balloons. Ask them to figure out the best way to get the compliments out of the balloons so that they can read them.

Now everyone may blow up his/her own balloon and tie it. After this you may allow each person to pop his/her own balloon and read the compliments that are found inside.

Discussion Prompts
1. How do you feel after reading the positive comments found in your balloon?
2. Do you believe these compliments? Why or why not?
3. Is it easier to give and receive compliments anonymously or directly? Why?

TRAIT TRACING

It is easy to compare ourselves to others and to believe we aren't good enough if we don't measure up to the people we admire. Only when we recognize our own unique traits and value as a person and stop trying to be somebody else can we begin to build a good self-esteem and a strong sense of who we are.

Objective
To help people recognize how they are different from other people and to discovery how this awareness can help them define their unique qualities and develop self-esteem.

Who
People who have difficulty realizing what their own unique traits are and who need to improve their own self-esteem.

Group Size
6 or more

Materials
- ➲ Paper
- ➲ Pens or pencils

Description
Challenge everyone in the group to find traits in each other that are different from their own. Ask everyone to take a piece of paper and pen or pencil and to make a list of their own unique traits.

Give the group a time limit (based on how many people are in the group) and ask them to go around and talk to each other. On the piece of paper each person must write down as many traits from other people in the group as s/he can find that are different from his/her own unique traits. The person with the longest list at the end of the time limit wins.

Discussion Prompts

1. Why is it important to find traits in each other that are different and unique?
2. What would life be like if we were all exactly the same?
3. How can you use your unique traits to build on and improve your self-esteem?

FLOWER PETALS

The more flower petals a flower has the bigger and brighter it is. Each petal by itself is a beautiful creation but when put together with other petals a complete flower is created.

Compliments are like flower petals. One compliment is wonderful but to receive many is a gift that can build a person up and make them glow from the inside out.

Objective
To increase positive feelings of people in the group by giving and receiving compliments.

Who
People with a low self-esteem who could benefit from hearing and accepting compliments from others.
Group members should be familiar with each other.

Group Size
3 to 9 is ideal

Materials
- Colored paper
- White paper
- Scissors
- Glue
- Pens or pencils
- Colored markers, crayons or pencils

Description
Give each person a piece of white paper and ask them to select some of the colored paper to be used to make a paper flower. Each person must cut out a stem and at least two leaves and glue these to the

paper with enough room on top for a flower. Each person must then write one thing that they like about themselves on each leaf of their own flower.

The next step is for each person to cut out flower petals for their flower (one for each of the other members of the group, two if the group is small). Each person should put his/her name on the back of each flower petal and then give one of the petals to each of the other members of the group. Instruct the group members that they are to write a positive comment or compliment on each petal and then return it to its owner.

After all the petals have been returned to each person, they may glue them to their flower stem so that all the positive comments can be seen.

Discussion Prompts

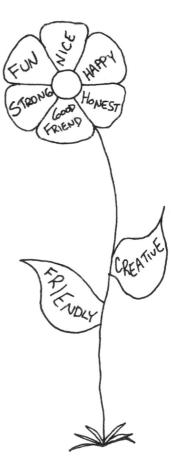

1. Was it harder to give yourself compliments or to give them to others? Why?
2. How does it feel to get positive comments from others?
3. Is it easier for you to say positive comments to others, or to write them down?
4. Why is it important to give compliments to others?
5. How can it help you to be more positive towards others?

TEN SECONDS

Have you ever talked to someone who is unhappy about life and who constantly says negative things? The sad thing is that these people need friends but may be pushing people away by the words that they choose. Getting people to think positively about the world, their own lives, and most importantly about themselves is a big step towards building a healthy and happy self-esteem.

Objective
To build up self-esteem and to create a positive atmosphere by saying and hearing positive comments.

Who
People who could benefit from hearing positive comments and who need to learn to be more positive with their talk.

Group Size
4 to 30 participants

Materials
➲   A watch, clock or timing device that can measure ten seconds

Description
Gather the group into a circle and ask for a volunteer to start the game. This person has ten seconds to say something positive, nice, complimentary, or uplifting. These comments can be about anything, or you may limit the comments to be about the group, group members, and/or the individual giving the comment.

After the positive comment has been given, the next person in the circle gets ten seconds to come up with his/her own positive comment, and so on around the circle. If at any time someone doesn't say something nice they are "out". You may also get "out" if you say a positive comment that has already been stated before in the game or if you say something negative during your ten seconds. Play elimination style or you may add the rule that once eliminated you may return to the activity once two other people say something nice to you. To change the difficulty level change the amount of time by adding or subtracting seconds.

Discussion Prompts
1. Was it hard or easy for you to come up with positive comments?
2. Do you usually say negative words to others or positive? Why?
3. What is the effect of positive words on a group?
4. How can positive words affect your everyday life?
5. Do you need to hear more positive words or say them more?

THREE FOR ME

The purpose of many games is to hit a target. The more the target gets hit the more points scored. In this game, if you miss the target, you're just as much a winner as you are when you hit it.

Sometimes winning isn't about getting the most points but about hearing the right encouragement from the sideline and feeling good about yourself because of what was said.

Objective
For people to show the ability to accept compliments from others and to be able to give compliments. For people to make positive statements about themselves.

Who
People who don't hear or give positive comments very often but who could benefit from this.

Group Size
4 to 20 participants

Materials
- ⊃ Frisbee®
- ⊃ Hula Hoop (or any type of target)
- ⊃ Soccer ball
- ⊃ Two orange cones, boundary markers or a soccer goal
- ⊃ Two large sheets of paper and two fat tipped markers
- ⊃ Stopwatch or timer

Description
Engage the group in the following three activities (one after the other:
1. FRISBEE THROW: Lean a hula-hoop up against a wall or other stable surface. Each person takes a turn throwing the Frisbee at the

target from a pre determined spot. If the Frisbee goes in the hoop, the individual who threw it must say one nice thing about him/herself; if the target is missed, then the individual must point to anyone else in the group and that person must then say something nice about the individual.

2. SOCCER SHOT: Set up a soccer goal that is somewhat challenging but not too difficult. Each person takes a turn and attempts to make a goal from a pre-determined spot. If the shooter makes a goal, then everyone in the group must say something nice about him/her. If the person misses the goal, then s/he must say something nice about the next person in line.

3. WRITE AND RUN: Divide the group into two teams and instruct each team to form a single file line. Set a large piece of paper and fat tipped marker at the other end of the room from each team. Give the group a three-minute time limit and inform them that this is a race to see which team can come up with the highest number of positive things written on their paper. The way that this is accomplished is for the first person in each line to run to his/her team's paper and write down something that s/he is good at doing or a special quality that s/he has. Once they have written something down they leave the pen by the paper, run back to their line and tag the next person who then does the same thing. The team must rotate through as many times as they can in the time limit in order to get more words written than the other team. After the race is over bring both teams together and look at how many things the group was able to list.

Discussion Topics

1. Did anyone feel uncomfortable today for any reason? If so, why?
2. How did it feel to get compliments?
3. How did you feel when giving compliments?
4. Was it easier to give and receive compliments during a game than in real life? Why?

COMMUNICATION SKILLS

E-mail, answering machines, the telephone, and a purchased card are the modern ways of communicating with one another. It is easy to maintain work relationships and casual acquaintances and to begin to build deeper relationships through these channels of communication. However, when thoughts and feelings are shared face to face, two people can bond at a deeper level, become closer to each other, and build a truly strong friendship.

Face to face communication can be a fun time of sharing information, stories and memories; when people open up to each other, a deeper relationship begins to form. Sharing feelings with others is often the most difficult type of communication, but it is also the most healing and relationship building.

In therapy, communication is often the main focus. When a person shares his/her feelings with a therapist, when two people work out their differences by talking, and when someone shares his/her emotional hurts and pains, the process of healing begins. The bottom line in most therapy sessions is getting people to communicate more effectively whether it be with the therapist or with another person.

Communication is more than just getting people to share their feelings; it is also about improving listening and verbal skills. To be successful in life, people need to communicate clearly and to listen and to understand what is said. Listening to directions and being able to follow these directions is particularly important for children. Special education classes are full of kids who have difficulty paying attention to what is said and who don't follow directions. The amazing thing is that when some of these same kids play a game, they have no problem following the directions. When this amazing and sudden ability to follow directions is pointed out to them, there is a good lesson to be learned. The lesson of selective listening is an effective and powerful way that games can be used as a therapeutic tool when teaching communication skills.

Games also can be used to open doors for the communication of feelings, to get people to talk with one another, to enhance social skills, and to practice verbal and listening skills. Of course games can do all of these things and be fun at the same time!

COMMUNICATION SKILLS GAMES AND ACTIVITIES

STORY STORY

To hear somebody say something and to actually listen to what is being said are two completely different things. Some people have a difficult time paying attention to what is said. They hear the voice but do not remember the words, and when at school or work, this can get them into trouble. This game gives people the chance to practice using good listening skills and to practice remembering what is said.

Objective
For individuals to show good listening skills and to show the ability to remember what they have heard.

Who
People who have difficulty listening and paying attention to whoever is talking.

Group Size
1 or more

Materials
- ➲ A short story book
- ➲ Game materials - varied

Description
Select a short story to be read to the group. Instruct the group to listen carefully to the story as you read it but offer no further instructions. Once you have read the story and put the book aside, inform the group that you will now play a game.

The game you select may be anything from an active gym game to a sit down board game. Play the game for only about five to ten minutes before quitting. After the game is played, read the story to the group again. Only this time stop at the end of each page and ask the group members to raise their hands if they can remember what happens on the next page. Allow them to guess what is next before turning the page.

This is a good test of listening skills and a good lesson on how much people really pay attention to what they hear!

Discussion Prompts
1. Was it easy or difficult for you to remember what was in the story? Why?
2. What does it mean "To hear someone"?
3. What does it mean "To listen to someone"?
4. What can you do to help yourself to remember what has been said?
5. Why is it important to listen to others?
6. How do you know when others are truly listening to you?

Variation
➲ For adults or more mature groups select a poem to read instead of a short story.

SOUNDS AROUND

At any given time there are many, many "sounds around" that can be heard by the human ear. Some people can focus on the single sound that they need to be paying attention to, (like the teacher's voice), while others are easily distracted by sounds that are unimportant and may miss out on the information that someone else is giving to them.

Objective
For people to recognize how much they really listen to and hear the sounds around them. To understand how important it is to listen to one sound without being distracted by all the other different sounds that are occurring at the same time.

Who
People who are easily distracted by sounds that they hear and who have trouble focusing on the one sound or person that they need to listen to.

Group Size
1 or more

Materials
- Paper
- Pen or pencil

Description
The leader has a piece of paper and a pen or pencil so s/he can make a list of all the sounds that the group hears. Start out inside if possible and ask the group to listen carefully and identify any sounds they hear. The leader then adds each new sound mentioned to the list. Then go outside if possible and continue to add to the list while taking a walk. After ten to twenty minutes of this activity you will probably have quite an extensive list.

Gather the group together for discussion afterwards and discuss the wide variety of sounds that are constantly going on around us and how difficult it may be to focus on one important sound at a time.

Discussion Prompts

1. Were you surprised by the number of sounds you heard?
2. Did you hear sounds today that you don't usually notice?
3. What is the difference between <u>hearing</u> something or someone and <u>listening</u> to someone or something?
4. How can you focus on one sound when there are many different sounds going on around you at one time?
5. Do you feel that you are a good listener? Why or why not?
6. How can you keep from being distracted by all of the different sounds going on around you at one time?

MYSTERY OBJECT

When you walk up to two people who are engaged in conversation, it is natural to be curious about the topic of conversation. You could interrupt and ask the pair "what are you talking about?" but this is not proper and considered to be poor manners. The other way to determine the topic being discussed is to listen to the details and to then figure out what is being talked about before joining in the conversation.

Objective
For participants to show good listening skills when listening to a conversation.

Who
People who need to work on their ability to listen carefully to what is said so they can increase their understanding of the information given to them.

Group Size
4 or more

Materials
➲ None

Description
Select two individuals who must secretly select an object in the room. In attempt to get the rest of the group to guess what the object is, they must carry on a conversation about the object without directly saying what it is. Meanwhile the rest of the group is listening and attempting to identify the mystery object.

Once the group has correctly guessed the object, select two more individuals to select a new object and start a new conversation.

Discussion Prompts

1. What did you have to do in order to figure out what the object was?
2. Were you able to detect what the word was by reading body language?
3. When is it important to listen to others?
4. Why should you listen carefully to others when they are talking?

Variations

➲ Select <u>anything</u> to talk about rather than just an object in the room.
➲ Write down different objects on paper and allow each pair to draw a slip of paper and discuss the object written down.

CRAZY SENTENCE

Listening to details can be very important when trying to solve a problem or when attempting to follow complicated directions. Sometimes the details are not essential but at other times these details are the most important part of the information being conveyed.

Being able to listen carefully to what is said and to all the words that a person is saying isn't an easy task. Sometimes we must listen with our eyes and observe body language, facial expressions, and eye movement in order to get all the information needed. The better you "listen" to the details, the more you will hear and the better you will understand what is being said.

Objective
To use good listening skills in order to win the game.

Who
People who need to work on their ability to listen carefully to what is said so they can increase their understanding of the information given.

Group Size
4 or more

Materials
➲ Paper
➲ Pens or pencils
➲ 2 Chairs

Description
Prior to this activity make up a dozen or so sentences that are complete and correct but make them crazy and random; then write each sentence on a small piece of paper. Some examples of crazy sentences are:

"My prom date had a large tattoo."

"Big Bird is my idol."

"The blue cow swam over the moon."

"It is good to eat spiders and caterpillars for breakfast."

"Rubber bands stick to the ceiling on Christmas day."

Be creative and come up with many more. Also, prior to the game set up two chairs in the front of the room.

For the activity select two people from the group and ask them to sit in the chairs that you have set up in the front of the room. Give each person a piece of paper with one of the crazy sentences on it. The two players must read the sentence to themselves and then engage in conversation. Each player attempts to state his/her sentence in the course of conversation. The object is to slip in the sentence without the other person guessing what it is. You may wish to give them a topic to start with such as fishing, country music, bowling, buying shoes, or anything else that has nothing to do with the sentences. Also give them a one or two minute time limit to slip their sentences in during the conversation. After the time limit, allow the people in the audience to guess what the crazy sentence is and whoever guesses correctly is given the opportunity to play the game for the next round.

Discussion Prompts

1. What did you have to do in order to detect the hidden sentence?
2. When do you use your best listening skills? Why?
3. When is it important for you to show good listening skills?

Variations

➲ Each player may tell a story, instead of engaging in conversation with one other player.

➲ This game can be done with three people engaging in conversation at the same time instead of just two.

➲ Play in teams and allow each team to make up sentences for the other team to use when telling a story to their own team.

CLOTHESPIN COUNT

Interrupting someone when they are talking is rude and a bad habit. Unfortunately it is a habit that many children have, and until they are taught differently, they may continue with this habit on into their adult lives. In this game people have to work extra hard at using proper communication skills, and some people must especially be aware of their desire to interrupt someone who is talking.

Objective
To become aware of different communication skills and how these skills affect the way we speak and listen to others.

Who
People who often interrupt others when they are talking, who blurt out comments at inappropriate times or who often say rude comments to others.

Group Size
3 or more

Materials
➲ A bag of clothespins
➲ Game materials - varied

Description
Select a game for the group to play (a sit down board game, card game, or guessing game works best). Before explaining the rules give each person two clothespins to put anywhere on their clothes. Inform the group that each person's job during the game is to try to keep their own clothespins. A clothespin may be taken away by anyone who catches someone else using poor communication skills: interrupting someone who is talking, blurting out of turn, making rude or

inappropriate comments, not showing good listening skills (for those who pay more attention to getting clothespins than they do to the rules of the game), etc. You may add more things to the list based on the skills your group needs to work on. (The leader may have to determine if a clothespin should be lost or not).

After explaining the clothespin rules, explain the rules of the game you have selected (a good opportunity for people to lose clothespins). Play the game and continue with the clothespin rule on into the discussion part as well. You may wish to give a prize to the person/s with the most clothespins at the end for added incentive.

Discussion Prompts

1. Why did you lose or keep your clothespins?
2. Why do people interrupt others who are talking?
3. How do you feel when others interrupt you when you are talking?
4. Why is it bad to interrupt others while they are talking?
5. What can you do to keep yourself from blurting out or interrupting people when they are talking?
6. How can you show others that you are listening to them when they are talking?

DARE DIRECTIONS

A dare is a challenge with no reward. The only reason people follow a dare is to prove themselves to the person giving the dare or to gain a sense of accomplishment from successfully living up to the challenge. A dare is usually something that is just beyond what you think your capabilities are (or in some cases your stupidity). In this game the dare is a challenge you give yourself and the more you challenge yourself the more you can learn.

Objective
To listen clearly to simple directions and follow them. To give clear understandable directions to others.

Who
People who have difficulty following one or multiple step directions.

Group Size
2 or more

Materials
➲ None

Description
Start by selecting one person to go first. This person then "dares" one of the other group members to give him/her a number of one step directions. For example: if it were Amy's turn she might say to Eric "Eric, I dare you to give me three directions to follow". Then Eric would say "I dare you to 1. Turn in a circle, 2. Give someone a 'high five', and 3. Do a push up." Amy would then have to listen carefully to the directions, remember what they are and then attempt to follow them accurately. Select a new person to "dare" someone else to give him/her directions after each turn.

Give points for good listening, and speaking skills. One point to someone if they give <u>clear</u> directions, two points to anyone who follows all the directions given to him/her, one point for anyone who follows the directions given to someone else (they may do them along with the person who has been given the directions). At the end give two bonus points to the person who follows the highest number of directions given.

Discussion Prompts

1. Was it easy for you to follow the directions given to you? Why or why not?
2. Do you ever have trouble following directions? Why?
3. What happens when you don't follow directions?
4. If it is difficult for you to follow directions, what can you do to make it easier?

COME FOLLOW ME

When you are giving directions for a game or for anything else, it is easy to think that the directions are clear until you actually see others try to follow them. At this point it may become apparent that the directions you gave were not so clear after all or that the people listening to them were not paying attention. In this activity, by playing a simple but fun game, everyone gets the chance to test their direction giving skills and to show their ability to follow directions given by someone else.

Objective
To communicate clear directions to others. To show the ability to listen and to follow directions.

Who
People who need to work on their ability to follow directions and who need to practice giving clear directions to others.

Group Size
4 to 16 participants

Materials
➲ Any equipment available that can be used to create an obstacle course (i.e. balls, cones, jump ropes, hula hoops, scooters, etc.)

Description
For this activity you need a large open room or gym that is divided into four sections (tape on the floor can work). Break up the group into four small groups (or allow each person to work on his/her own). Assign each group to a section and divide the available equipment among the groups.

Instruct each group to create a portion of an obstacle course with the supplies they have and in their section of the room. After each group has finished the task of creating part of the obstacle course in their own section, have an obstacle tour. On the tour each group explains their part of the course to the rest of the group and tells the other group members what they must do in order to navigate this part of the course. It is important for everyone to try and give very clear explanations of what they have created and for everyone else to listen carefully to all the directions. After the "tour" allow each person to go through the course, one section at time, so that they go through all the sections to finish the complete obstacle course. One person may go at a time or three or four different people, each starting at a different section, may all go at the same time.

The most important part is listening to the directions and showing that you can remember what you have heard by doing the correct things in each part of the course!

Discussion Prompts

1. Was it easy or hard to give clear directions to others? Why?
2. Was it easy or hard to listen to and follow all the directions given to you?
3. Do you ever have trouble following directions correctly? Why do you think this happens?
4. Why is it important to be able to follow directions?

CRAZY COMIC

Creating a good concept can take a really long time, and lots of thought must be put into it. When there is a large group of people working on the idea, the task may suddenly become easier because there is more brainpower working on the project. However, if people can't communicate their ideas with each other and make group decisions, many problems may arise. This activity is a simple task, but a great deal of communication is needed if a group is to be successful when attempting to work together to create an original idea.

Objective
To communicate ideas with others and make group decisions based upon discussion.

Who
People who need to work on communicating ideas with other people and who need to learn how to make a group decision by compromising on the ideas given.

Group Size
3 or more

Materials
- Paper
- Pens or pencils
- Colored markers, crayons, or colored pencils

Description
Divide the group into smaller groups of three to six members each. Supply each person in each group with a piece of paper and writing utensil. Instruct the groups that they are to create an original comic strip and each person in the group must draw one frame of the strip (if

there are four people in a group, the comic strip will contain four frames). The group must decide what to draw, the story line and who will draw what (there is a lot of communication involved in this one)!

Once the discussion has taken place about the comic strip and the decisions have been made, each person draws the frame s/he is responsible for on his/her own piece of paper. Everyone should be drawing at the same time and not taking turns with their group members. If you want to make it really challenging, don't allow group members to see each others' papers when they are drawing.

After the comic strips are completed, allow time for sharing and give each group a chance to show their comic strip to the other groups.

Discussion Prompts

1. What different communication skills were needed for this activity?
2. How important was communication during this activity?
3. What was the most difficult part of this activity for you?
4. Did your comic strip flow? Why or why not?
5. When involved in part of a group process, do you want things to always go your way or do you allow others to contribute ideas?
6. Why is it important to be able to make decisions with other people?
7. What things do you need to do when making decisions with others?
8. In your life, when is it important to be able to communicate clearly with others?

Variation

➲ Give them some ideas about what characters or settings to use in the comic strips.

BLiND SCULPTURE

Giving clear directions is sometimes difficult, but with the help of hand motions and body language, it can be made easier. Giving directions quickly becomes more difficult when the communication is strictly verbal and the nonverbal communication is taken away as it is in this simple but fun game.

Objective
To recognize the importance of using good communication skills when giving and receiving directions.

Who
People who need to work on communicating their thoughts and ideas in a clear, organized manner. People who need to improve their ability to listen to others and follow directions.

Group Size
2 or more (an even number works best)

Materials
- Building toys - i.e. blocks, Tinkertoys®, Legos®, Popsicle® sticks, etc.
- Sheet
- Rope
- Two chairs

Description
Set up the two chairs across the room with the rope tied between them and the sheet draped over the rope to create a wall. Divide the group into pairs and ask them to sit on the ground across from their partner, with the wall dividing them.

Give everyone a hand full of identical building toys/materials. Ask the people on one side of the wall to build a small structure or design with what you have given them. After they have finished building, ask them to verbally explain to their partner how to precisely build the sculpture. The partner then attempts to build it to look like the original by listening to the directions of the original builder. Once everyone has completed their sculptures, remove the sheet and let them compare the original sculptures to the copies. Allow each partner to participate in the different roles of this activity by switching the roles of original builders and listeners.

Discussion Prompts
1. Was it easier for you to give directions or to receive directions? Why?
2. Do you usually follow directions given to you? Why or why not?
3. Do you feel people listen to you when you tell them what you want them to do?
4. Why is it important to be able to listen to others and follow the directions they have given you?
5. What do you do in your everyday life to show that you are using good listening skills?

DUCKS FLY

Paying close attention to directions, listening, and responding to someone who is talking are all important parts of following directions and using good listening skills (especially for young children). This game puts those skills to the test in a fun way and helps children improve their listening skills in the process.

Objective
To keep from becoming "it" by listening carefully.

Who
Children who have difficulty listening and paying attention to whoever is talking.

Group Size
3 or more

Materials
➲ None

Description
Select someone to be "it" and ask s/he to stand in front of the group. This person calls out "Ducks fly!, Seagulls fly!, Ladybugs fly!, Cows fly!". Whenever "it" says an animal that flies, everyone flaps their wings in a flying motion. As soon as s/he says an animal that doesn't fly, then everyone should stop "flying" and put their arms down to their sides. Whoever keeps "flying" when a non-flying animal is mentioned is eliminated. The game should keep going until one person remains who then gets to be "it" for the next round.

The person who is "it" can say any animals they think of, not just the ones listed, or use animals that jump, crawl, roar, etc.

Discussion Prompts

1. What did you have to do in this game if you wanted to become "it"?
2. When and why do you have to listen carefully to directions?
3. Is it easy or hard for you to listen carefully to others? Why?
4. What can you do to help yourself listen to others and follow directions?

Variation

➲ Instead of being eliminated when you don't listen, you become "it".

VERBAL ORIGAMI

Giving directions is an easy task when you can demonstrate the directions. When only words are used, the task of giving and of following directions can become more difficult and confusing for all those involved. Without the physical demonstration, good verbal and excellent listening skills are of utmost importance, as you will see in this challenging activity.

Objective
To listen carefully to directions and show the ability to follow them. To give clear directions to others.

Who
People who need to learn to give clear directions and who need to learn how to receive and understand directions that are given to them.

Group Size
2 or more

Materials
- Paper (optional: origami paper)
- Simple origami (Japanese paper folding art) book/directions (or) paper airplane directions

Description
Supply each person in the group with a piece of paper. Select one person to come to the front of the room who must explain to the others how to fold the paper into the shape of an object, animal or paper airplane. The person explaining the directions needs to get his/her information from directions found in a book or another source of written directions. The explanation must be purely verbal, with no

physical demonstration allowed. The direction giver may not tell the others what it is that they are creating but may describe it.

This is a difficult activity since many of the directions given in books involve diagrams. It may be used for a wide variety of functioning levels if altered enough (see variations). Allow people to take turns giving the directions so more people get to experience both sides of this activity (breaking them into smaller groups is a good way to allow everyone to both give and receive directions).

Discussion Prompts

1. Was it more difficult for you to give or to receive directions? Why?
2. Did anyone ever feel frustrated at any time during this activity? Why or why not?
3. Do you ever have trouble understanding what it is that someone is trying to tell you? What do you do to help them?
4. Do you feel others always understand what it is you are trying to say?
5. Do your feelings ever get misunderstood? Why do you think that is?
6. Why is it important to be able to communicate information clearly?

Variations

➲ Take one person out of the room and show him/her how to fold a piece of paper. S/he must watch carefully and return to the group and explain the folds made. This process may be as simple as folding the paper in half with a corner folded down (but in no particular shape at all).
➲ Participants may or may not ask questions of the person who is giving the directions.

WHAT'S DIFFERENT?

Have you ever been talking to someone and felt like s/he was not listening to a word you were saying? The biggest clue people give that they are not paying attention is to look at anything or anyone except for the person who is talking.

People who have difficulty listening to others or paying attention to instructions are often easily distracted, as shown by their lack of eye contact. Listening skills can be improved by simply becoming aware of distractions and by practicing good eye contact.

Objective
To practice using eye contact and observation skills when listening to others.

Who
People who need to learn to use good eye contact when listening to others. People who need to learn to observe body language when listening to someone who is talking to them.

Group Size
3 or more

Materials
➲ None

Description
Gather the group into a circle and ask for a volunteer to stand in the middle. Everyone must look closely at this person and try to remember what s/he is wearing and looks like. This person leaves the room and changes something observable about his/her appearance (i.e. roll up the sleeves of a shirt, take out earrings, switch a watch from one arm to the other, etc.). When s/he returns to the room, everyone tries to guess

what is different. Whoever guesses is the next person to leave the room and change something about his/her appearance.

Emphasize the need to look carefully at the person to determine what is different. When people are distracted by other things in the room and not being observant, this activity is much more difficult, just as paying attention to someone who is talking is difficult when the listener is distracted by something else.

Discussion Prompts

1. What did you have to do if you wanted to be able to guess what was different?
2. How does this compare to what you have to do when you are listening to someone who is speaking to you?
3. How do you feel when you are talking to someone and they aren't looking at you?
4. Do you give others good eye contact when they are talking to you? Why is it important to give good eye contact?
5. Can observing people help you listen to them better? If so, how?

TALK TO ME

When you receive directions to a specific location it is easy to find your way if there are only two or three steps to remember. When the directions are more complex and involve more steps, there is a greater chance of the person following them getting lost. The challenge of this game is to listen carefully to directions that are more than one step and to not get lost along the way.

Objective
For individuals to be able to listen to directions and to show the ability to follow the directions that are given to them.

Who
People who need practice following simple directions.
People who need to practice following one or multiple step directions.

Group Size
4 or more

Materials
- Small slips of paper
- Pens or pencils

Description
Divide the group into two teams. Use the directions listed on the next page (or make up your own) and write each one down on a separate slip of paper. Fold each piece of paper in half so that the directions can not be seen and ask one member from the first team to come forward. This person unfolds the directions and reads it to the second team one time (and no more). The second team must wait for the direction to be read entirely and then as a group they must attempt to follow the exact directions given to them.

If everyone is successful in completing the direction, then the team receives one point, but if any of the team members does not follow the direction completely, there is no point earned for that round.

Allow the teams to go back and forth in this manner until all of the directions are used up. At this point each team must get together and create a new list of directions to be given to the opposite team. Each direction may have no more than three steps (maybe more for higher functioning groups) and must be something that the other team can do safely.

DIRECTIONS
1. Everyone has to give everyone else on your team a "high five" and then the whole team must sit in a circle.
2. Three people on your team must sing the alphabet and then the whole team must get in a huddle and yell "break".
3. Your team must form a line from shortest to tallest, then everyone must stay in the line and as a group jump up and down four times.
4. One person on your team must do five sit ups while the rest of the group cheers for this person while standing in a circle around him/her.

Discussion Prompts
1. Was it easy or difficult for you to follow all of the directions given to you?
2. Did your team help you follow the directions or hinder you? Why?
3. When is it important for you to listen to others and to follow directions?
4. How can you show others that you are listening to them when they are talking or giving you directions?

Variation
⊃ Add a step to each direction, starting with a simple two step direction, then give a three step direction, then four, five, etc. Challenge the group to see which team can do the most directions.

SECRET WORD

Some people have secret words that they keep hidden inside - words of hurt, anger, betrayal and/or confusion that need to be shared with someone else so that inner healing can begin to take place. Often times the words are hidden and the secrets are kept because communicating these secrets is a big risk and the words aren't so easy to say.

Objective
To encourage interactive conversation among group members and to help people openly discuss how they feel when talking about "secrets" from their own lives.

Who
People who need to practice engaging in appropriate, interactive conversation with others. People who need to be encouraged to open up to others through communication.

Group Size
3 or more

Materials
➲ None

Description
Select one person from the group to leave the room or to go away from the group so s/he can not hear their discussion. The remaining group members select a "secret" word (this can be any word). When the individual who left the room returns, everyone attempts to get this person to say the "secret" word.

The group may ask the person questions, engage the person in conversation or whatever else they can think of in order to get this person to say the "secret" word. The individual who doesn't know the word tries to talk as much as possible without saying the word.

Once the word has been said, select a new person to leave the room for another round of the game.

Discussion Prompts

1. Do you enjoy talking with other people?
2. Who do you like to talk with the most and why?
3. Do you wish you had more people in your life that you could talk to?
4. Do you wish you could talk about things in your life more easily?
5. Do people ever try to get you to say "secret" words? Who? Why?
6. Would it help you to talk about your "secrets" with others?
7. To whom would you tell your secrets and why?
8. Why don't you share your secrets with others?

ONE-TWO-THREE BREAK

In the game of basketball there are many plays that are executed during the course of a game. These plays are planned out and sometimes given a code name or signal so that everyone knows which play they should be doing and everyone can do their part to make it work. Creating plays involves group members communicating with each other. When the plays are used in the game, team members must be paying close attention to what their team members are doing and be able to listen and follow directions.

Objective
For group members to communicate with each other in order to make up directions and to communicate these directions to each other so that everyone is able to follow them.

Who
People who need to practice using communications skills when making group decisions. People who need to practice listening to and following directions.

Group Size
10 is ideal but a few more or less will work

Materials
- Basketball Court
- 2 basketballs

Description
Divide the group into two teams for a regular basketball game and play a game by regular rules. However before starting the game give each team a basketball, one half of the court and ten minutes time. Instruct the two teams that they have ten minutes to work together as a group to create three plays that they can use during the game and to

practice these plays as a team. Each play should have a word or signal that starts each play and should include all members of the team, who should know what their job is for the play. The plays can be as silly and crazy as each team wants to make them!

After the ten minutes gather the two teams together and play a game of basketball for a given amount of time and tell the teams that they must attempt each play at least once during the time period. Emphasize the use of listening skills, of being aware of everyone around them, and of following the directions that their team has created.

For added fun you may stop the game and give each team three minutes to get together in a huddle and to think of a cheer for their team. Then allow each team to yell their made up cheer before starting the game again.

Discussion Prompts

1. How was the communication on your team when you were creating your plays?
2. How important was it for you to listen during this activity?
3. What is the difference between not remembering a lot of information and not listening to information? Did you see either of these things happen today?

Variations

⊃ For lower functioning groups give them simple plays that they must learn and remember or limit the number of plays they have to do to one or two.
⊃ This activity will also work for football.

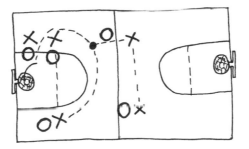

SELF-DISCOVERY

We all have a story to tell, a story of our experiences, memories, knowledge, and relationships. If we all had to write our stories, some people would have an easier time than others. A story of pain, frustration and sadness would find its way onto the pages of one story whereas happiness, fulfillment, and adventure might be found in another's. Either way there is much to be learned from each story, and the lessons learned can help people grow and learn so they can become a person full of great potential.

When writing your own stroy the hardest part is knowing the perspective of others. We often think we know how others see and perceive us, but the truth is that until we take the time to ask, we never really know. Learning how others see us is a big part of self-discovery and helps us build on our strengths and learn from our weaknesses.

People with low self-esteems often assume that others don't think very highly of them and have difficulty changing until they hear positive comments from others. People who have a confident demeanor may not be using their skills to their full potential until they are told what their strengths are and they can then focus on these. What others think is often hard to hear, and it is a big risk to give others compliments or constructive criticism.

People who go into therapy and who want or need to change the direction of their life stories can learn the most from others or by stepping back to take a look at their own lives. The biggest and the hardest step that needs to be taken if positive change is to occur is to figure out what changes need to be made. What are we currently doing that we can change so we can do it better? Hearing constructive criticism is difficult, but if it is given to you in a caring manner, it can be the best thing that ever happened to help you change your life story. People really do want to know how others see them, and self-discovery can become the greatest learning tool of all to bring about change and can lead to a story with a happy ending rather than one with a sad and tragic ending.

Not only is it important to be able to hear and give constructive criticism to others, but we must also give it to ourselves. We must be able to accept our own self-discoveries so we can learn, grow and change our own stories that we are constantly in the process of writing!

SELF-DISCOVERY GAMES AND ACTIVITIES

ACTION EMOTIONS

Emotions encompass a wide range of feelings, and the way that people express these different emotions varies greatly from person to person. Some people are quite dramatic, and it is always easy to tell what they are feeling, while others are quiet and reserved, leaving people to guess how they are feeling. For the dramatic, this activity will be easy, but for the reserved ones, it may take some stretching and the challenge to go beyond one's own comfort zone in order to grow and learn.

Objective
To show the ability to express a wide variety of emotions and to be able to recognize emotions that are expressed by others.

Who
People who have difficulty expressing their emotions.
People who have difficulty recognizing and reacting to the emotions of others.

Group Size
4 or more

Materials
- Pens or pencils
- Paper

Description
Break the group up into smaller teams of two to six members each. Provide each team with a list of emotions (with at least enough for one per person) and a piece of paper with a place listed on it. For example, one team may get: happy, frustrated, jealous, scared and the place is a bowling alley.

Allow at least five minutes for each team to meet, look at their list, and create a skit. Each skit must contain all the emotions from the group's list, the emotions must be acted out, and the skit must take place at the given location. Also, each person must have a role in the skit that is created by his/her own group. At the end of the five minutes, gather the groups back together and allow time for each group to present their skit. At the end of each skit, those who were watching guess what emotions were being acted out.

Discussion Prompts

1. Is it easy for you to show your emotions? Why or why not?
2. Does anyone wish that others around them would show their emotions more or less? Why?
3. Why is it important to let others know how you are feeling?
4. Are there times when it is better for you to hide how you feel? Why?
5. What can you do to let others know how you feel (if they can't tell by your body language)?

BARE FEET

Your feet move you ahead one step at a time. In life people must move forward one step at a time by making goals and by working hard to achieve those goals. This activity combines goal making and the reality of taking one step at a time towards achieving those goals.

Objective
To set goals and to make a commitment to reaching these goals.

Who
People who need to change their lives so that they can better themselves and who need to set positive, realistic goals for themselves as a part of this process.

Group Size
1 or more

Materials
- ➲ Plaster of Paris
- ➲ Pie pans
- ➲ Paper plates
- ➲ Or washable paints and paper

Description
Using either plaster and pie pans or washable paints and paper make an individual footprint of each person in the group. Each person then writes or paints at least one individual goal they have for their own life next to their own footprint. The goals should focus on "where you want to go in your life".

Talk about how your feet take you places and move you ahead and relate it to how goals can be reached if you move forward with your life.

Discussion Prompts
1. Are these goals realistic for you?
2. Why is it important to set goals for yourself?
3. Do you have any other goals that you want to strive for?
4. What arc you doing right now to accomplish your goals?

Variation
⊃ May be done with a stamp pad and it is great if you can emboss each footprint (a technique you can find information about in many craft or rubber stamp stores)!

THE WAY WE WERE

A song on the radio, a name, a sound - these are all things that can bring up long forgotten memories from the past. Sometimes these memories are about a difficult time in life that someone went through. At other times the things remembered are happy, wonderful and something worth hanging onto. This activity brings sounds and memories together as a way of helping people open up and to help them share about their lives.

Objective
For people to realize how the environment around them affects their feelings and to recognize how they react to the sounds that they hear.

Who
People who need prompting in order to talk about their thoughts and feelings.

Group Size
1 or more

Materials
- Tape player
- Blank tape
- Paper
- Pens or pencils

Description
Prior to the activity make a tape recording of a wide variety of sounds and noises (i.e. car motor, baby crying, toilet flushing, washing machine, wind in the trees, etc.). For the activity give each person paper and a pen or pencil. Instruct them that they are to listen to each sound and to write down any feeling that the sound evokes in them or

104 ACTIVITIES THAT BUILD

any memories they have when they hear the sound. After the tape is finished allow individuals to read the feelings that they have written down to the rest of the group.

Discussion Prompts

1. Which sound produced the most negative feelings for you, the most positive feelings for you? Why?
2. Do any sounds bring up past memories for you? What?
3. In your life arc you surrounded by mainly positive sounds or mostly negative sounds?
4. If surrounded by negative sounds, how can you change the environment that you are in?

Variation

➲ Ask people to draw, color or paint pictures as they listen to the sounds, based on what they feel or remember.

POSSIBLE PREDICTIONS

Knowing what you want in life and striving to get there will keep you motivated, and the more you work towards your goals the more likely you are to reach them. People who don't have goals or who can't picture themselves doing anything positive with their lives often end up right where they expected and they may feel unhappy and unfulfilled. Getting people to think about their future is an important step towards creating a good one.

Objective
To learn more about how others in the group view us. To get feedback from others on the potential that we possess and to think about how our lives can change for the better.

Who
People who need to set goals for themselves and set standards to work towards in their own lives.

Group Size
2 or more

Materials
➲ Paper
➲ Pens or pencils

Description
Ask each person in the group to write his/her name on the bottom of a piece of paper and to write the three following categories: five years, ten years, twenty years, above his/her name with lines going up to the top of the page between each category. Ask everyone to put their papers into a pile in the middle of the group so that everyone can reach them.

Instruct the group that they are to take one paper at a time and on the top of the page make a prediction about what they think that person will be doing in the years to come, with one prediction for each category. The predictions should be positive and reflect the positive attributes of each person.

Once predictions are made from one person, the top of the paper should be folded over so the next person will not know what has been previously written and will not be influenced so that each prediction will be unique. Instruct group members to place the paper back into the pile when they are finished writing and take a different one; people may or may not write their names next to the comments they have written. Everyone should get the chance to write on everyone else's paper before the activity is over. Once all of the predictions have been made, allow time for everybody to read their papers to themselves.

Discussion Prompts
1. Would you have made the same predictions for yourself, or something different?
2. Do any of the predictions surprise you? If so, why?
3. Are there any predictions on your paper that you will consider pursuing?
4. What have you learned about yourself from this activity?

Variations
- ➲ Instead of encouraging positive predictions ask for realistic predictions based on the way the person is living his/her life right now. This can be a good way to open people's eyes to the negative paths they seem to be taking now.
- ➲ Have people write predictions for themselves and compare to the predictions that other people write for them.

CREATIVE COOKIES

Allowing someone else to know what you are feeling is sometimes a scary thing and can leave you feeling vulnerable. However, when the hurt and loneliness are not shared the pain will only deepen. The hardest way to open up to others is to directly tell them how you are feeling, but if done in writing or through symbols, the process of opening up to others can be made easier.

Objective
To recognize how each person is unique, special and different from everyone else and to explore feelings around giving a part of yourself to someone else through personal sharing and thus being left vulnerable.

Who
People who have a difficult time sharing how they are feeling with those around them.

Group Size
3 or more

Materials
- Pre-made sugar cookies in different shapes
- Different colors of frosting
- A variety of cookie decorating items i.e. sprinkles, candy, frosting tubes, etc.
- Spreading knives
- Plastic wrap

Description
Spread out all of the cookie decorating supplies on a table and allow each person to select two of the cookies. Ask participants to decorate

one cookie in a way that is representative of how they are feeling (by selecting colors of frosting, types of candy, specific shaped cookie, designs, etc.) and to save this cookie. The other cookie is for eating and can be decorated any way they wish.

Once everyone has completed making their cookies, ask them to show their cookies to the group and to explain how the cookie is representative of how they are feeling. Have each person wrap his/her cookie in plastic wrap and then ask them to give their cookie to someone who they feel they can trust with their feelings (this person may or may not be a member of the group). Challenge them to tell that person what their cookie means and to tell them why they chose that person to give it to.

If possible at a later meeting allow time for people to share with the group who they gave their cookie to, what happened, and how they felt.

Discussion Prompts

1. Will it be difficult for you to give your cookie away? Why or why not?
2. Do you ever have difficulty sharing your feelings with others or opening up to others? Why do you think this is?
3. Do you wish people close to you would be more open about how they feel? If not, why? If so, who and why?

Variation

↪ Have the group make the cookies from scratch prior to the group session as a teamwork activity. Each person should shape his/her own cookie in a way that is representative of him/her.

EMOTION BENCH

Actors exaggerate their emotions when they act so that the audience can easily capture the feelings they are trying to convey. Because people sometimes expect others to know how they are feeling and have trouble expressing their emotions like an actor can, they go through life feeling as if nobody truly understands them. This game is a fun way to practice acting out those emotions that many people keep hidden deep down inside.

Objective
To practice expressing feelings and emotions to others.

Who
People who have a difficult time expressing their emotions.
People who have a difficult time recognizing how others are feeling.

Group Size
4 or more

Materials
➲ 2 Chairs

Description
In front of the room set up two chairs next to each other and facing all of the participants who should be sitting on the floor, or in chairs, facing the front. Select two individuals to sit in the chairs and inform them that they are sitting on the "emotion bench".

Whisper a different emotion into the ear of each person who is sitting on the "bench". Each person must act out the emotion they have been given while those in the audience try to guess what emotion each person is acting out. The two on the bench are to engage in impromptu dialog, and the only rule is that someone must say "hi" first. Once dialog starts, the two people on the bench may be at a bus stop, at the movies, or wherever their imagination takes them. Allow the two to dialog for a while before asking the audience to guess the emotions. Those who guess correctly become the next participants to sit on the "emotion bench" (or they may select someone else to take a turn if they are uncomfortable with acting).

IDEAS FOR EMOTION BENCH LIST

Upset	-	Excited
Agitated	-	Assertive
Frustrated	-	Self-assured
In love	-	Angry
Nervous	-	Sad
Hyper	-	Insecure

Discussion Prompts

1. Was it easy to guess the emotions or difficult? Why?
2. Do you think people can easily read what emotions you are feeling?
3. Do you want others to know what you are feeling? Why or why not?
4. Can allowing others to know what you are feeling help you? How?
5. How can you find out what feelings and emotions others are experiencing?

EMOTIONS iN MOTION

Some people are easy to read: their emotions match their body language and words. Other people are harder to figure out, and it is difficult to detect what it is that they are feeling because they don't express their emotions with words or body language. There are times when it is appropriate for people to show and say how they are feeling because it is important that others know. However if people can't read the body language of a needy person it may be hard to react to him/her in a constructive way.

Objective
To show appropriate body language to coincide with a stated emotion and for people to practice showing emotions and sharing feelings.

Who
People who have a difficult time expressing their emotions.
People who have a difficult time recognizing how others are feeling.

Group Size
4 to 20 participants

Materials
➲ None

Description
Gather the group into a circle with everyone standing. Ask an individual to state an emotion and to act out this emotion through his/her body language (no words allowed). Then the next person in the circle acts out the same emotion in his or her own way. This continues around the circle until everyone has had an opportunity to show the emotion. Continue in this manner with different people choosing emotions that are to be passed around the circle.

Discussion Prompts

1. Is it ever hard for you to show your true emotions? Why?
2. Is it always easy to tell what someone is feeling by reading their body language?
3. What is the best way to find out how an individual is feeling?
4. Why is it important for our words to match our actions?

ViEWS

How a person views him/herself is often very different from how others view this same person. People often don't allow people to know what is going on on the inside. What people see on the outside isn't always an accurate picture of how a person is feeling and of all that they are going through. This is the reason for the different views of a person from the inside out.

Objective

For people to be able to express themselves in a nonverbal manner and to give people the opportunity to learn more about themselves and other members of the group.

Who

People who have a difficult time talking about their thoughts and feelings. People who need to understand themselves better so they can begin to take steps towards bettering their own lives.
Groups of people who could benefit from opening up to one another.

Group Size

1 or more

Materials

- One paper grocery bag per person
- Old magazines to cut pictures from
- Glue
- Colored markers
- Scissors
- Paper
- Pens or pencils

Description

Give everyone in the group a paper grocery bag and place all the other materials in the center of the table. Explain that "your bag represents yourself; on the outside you are to glue on magazine pictures, write words or draw pictures of how you think other people see you".

"On the inside put pictures or write down words on paper of how you see yourself". When everyone has completed their projects, encourage participants to share with the group as much as they feel comfortable sharing about their bags.

Discussion Prompts

1. What did you discover about yourself?
2. What did you learn about someone else in the group?
3. What is the easiest way for you to share your feelings? Why?

CD COVER

When people go to a music store, they spend time walking around looking at all of the selections and often will leave the store having bought a compact disk or two. The type of music a person buys and listens to can often times tell you quite a bit about that person. If each person made his/her own music recordings and designed the cover for the CD, others would probably learn much new information about the individual whose recording it is.

Objective
To think about your own life and feelings and to verbally share these thoughts with other people in the group.

Who
People who have difficulty sharing about their lives when in a group setting and who need prompting to do so openly.

Group Size
1 or more

Materials
- One piece of white tag board or cardboard per person (cut into about 8"x8" square)
- Colored markers, crayons, colored pencils, etc.
- Glitter, glue, stickers, ribbons or anything else available for use when decorating a cover

Description
Give each person a piece of white tag board or cardboard (about 8 inches by 8 inches). Supply the group with all of the other supplies mentioned above and inform them that they are to create their own CD (Compact Disk) Cover. On the cover they need to have a title for their

CD and any pictures or words that represent who they are. The CD cover is make believe and should be created and decorated with titles, songs, and pictures that represent the person who has created it. On the back they need to list the songs (real or make believe) that are on their CD. Side one should contain songs "about yourself" and on side two, songs about the "goals you have for yourself" (even though a real CD only has one side). After everyone is finished allow time for sharing.

Discussion Prompts
1. What was the hardest part of this activity for you? Why?
2. What did you learn about others in the group?
3. Do you think anyone should have a different title or different songs? Why?
4. Is it hard for you to recognize positive things in your life? Why?

FAMILY TOTEM POLE

A totem pole is a tall woodcarving consisting of animal heads and/or bodies and is used to tell Native American stories or legends. A family totem pole can be created to tell the story of a family in a fun and unique way.

Objective
For people to explore feelings, perceptions, and relationships that they have with their family members.

Who
People who need to share about their family life with the group or with a counselor but who have a difficult time talking about family dynamics and family situations.

Group Size
1 or more

Materials
- ➲ Construction Paper
- ➲ Glue
- ➲ Scissors
- ➲ Tape
- ➲ Colored markers
- ➲ Optional: Cardboard tube (i.e. toilet paper roll, paper towel roll or wrapping paper tube)
- ➲ Optional: Google eyes, felt, fabric, puff balls, pipe cleaners, or anything else that can be used to create animal faces.

Description
Ask the group if they know what a totem pole is and explain how each totem pole tells a unique story. Explain to the group that they are

to create their own unique totem poles about their families. Each person chooses a different animal to represent each family member and places the animal on the pole wherever they think that family member should be in their own story. For example, one pole may have a lion for a brother who is good looking, athletic and everything seems to come easy for him, and who also happens to be known for being quite lazy. Each totem pole must include at least three people and each person must put him/herself on the totem pole s/he is creating. Emphasize that a family can be whoever they feel their family is at the time. For some it may be a foster family, grandparents, a special relative, or even a group home.

Give each person a cardboard tube or create one by rolling construction paper long ways into a tube and taping it. Supply the group with all the animal face creation supplies that you have gathered that can be used to create animal faces. Instruct them to create animals out of the materials and to glue them onto their totem pole. Allow quite a bit of time for this activity and people will do a really good job and be proud of their totem poles when they are finished with them. Allow for sharing time at the end so that each person may explain his/her special family totem pole to the group.

Discussion Prompts
Discuss each totem pole after it has been explained to the group. You may allow group members to ask questions or use this time to discuss family relations that are occurring in each separate family.

Variation
➲ Create the totem poles out of modeling clay or play dough.

BOOK ABOUT ME

Any group of people that spends time together, works together or who are in therapy together could benefit from knowing more about one another. Sometimes it is hard to open up and share about yourself if people don't even know the simple day to day things in your life. Learning the likes, dislikes, recreation activities and the deeper details that others have in their lives can be the beginning of bringing a group of people together.

Objective
For people to think about their own lives and to share these thoughts with others.

Who
People who have difficulty sharing about their lives, family, likes, dislikes, etc. Groups of people who could benefit from getting to know more about one another.

Group Size
1 or more

Materials
- ➲ Paper
- ➲ Pens or pencils
- ➲ Colored markers, crayons, colored pencils, etc.
- ➲ Tape, staples or hole punch and yarn

Description
Supply the group with paper, drawing and writing supplies and ask them to create a "book about me". Give them the following list as a guideline for the book, with each topic on it's own page. Each page may contain pictures, words or anything else. After everyone has

finished, put the pages together in the form of the book with tape, staples or punch holes in the side and bind together with pieces of yarn. Then allow time for sharing.

1. What I look like
2. Things I do well
3. My favorite foods are
4. What my family looks like
5. My favorite place to go on vacation
6. What I am most proud of
7. My favorite thing to do on a rainy day
8. My favorite things to do with my family are
9. Things that make me sad
10. Things that make me happy

Discussion Prompts
Discuss each book after it has been shared.

CURIOUS CUBE

Each person in the world has many different sides: a happy side, sad side, scared side, family oriented side, free spirited side and more. Some people show their many different sides easily and frequently while others hide their many different feelings and only show one side. This is a simple project that allows people to show some of their many sides.

Objective
For people to think about and to share verbally with others about their own lives and for them to recognize many of the positive attributes that they possess.

Who
People who have trouble sharing their thoughts and feelings with others and who need a means to express themselves verbally.

Group Size
1 or more

Materials
- Construction Paper
- Tape
- Magazines
- Scissors
- Colored markers, crayons, or colored pencils
- Glue

Description
Have each participant create a cube out of the construction paper by cutting it in half the long way and folding each half into three sections and taping the sections to each other to form a cube (or build the cubes

the best way you know how). After each person has created a cube, instruct them to decorate each of the six sides with different pictures that are drawn or cut out of magazines and words that describe things about their life. As a guideline for the cube use the six following items to be covered (one for each side):

1. Things you are good at doing
2. Future dreams/plans
3. About your family
4. How you feel right now
5. Accomplishments you are proud of in your own life
6. What you like about yourself

Allow time for sharing after everyone is finished.

Discussion Prompts
Discuss each cube after it has been shared.

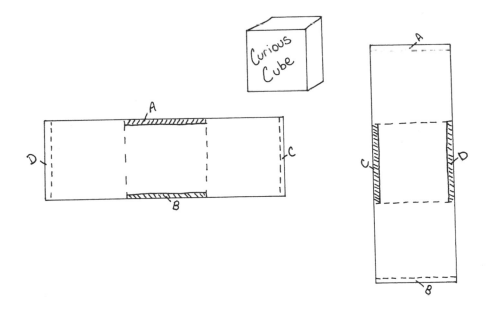

ST. BEDE SCHOOL
333 BERMUDA DR. N.W.
CALGARY, ALBERTA T3K 2J5
274-6243

PERSONAL FLAG

Each flag that is made has a story behind it. The colors, shapes, designs and pictures on a flag all represent something special. If each person had his/her own flag, each one would be unique and tell a special story of the person it represents.

Objective
To express yourself in a creative way and to share about your life with others in the group.

Who
People who have trouble sharing their thoughts and feelings with others and who need a means of expressing themselves verbally.

Group Size
1 or more

Materials
- Paper
- Pens or pencils
- Colored markers, crayons, or colored pencils
- Optional: glitter, glue, paint, fabric, scissors, or anything else you can find to decorate with

Description
For this activity each person makes a personal flag to represent who s/he is as a person. Each person must think of his/her own country name and chose colors, slogans and pictures that represent him/her to put on this personal flag. When everyone is finished allow time for sharing.

Discussion Prompts

1. Why did you choose what you did for your flag?
2. Each flag is unique; what do you think is unique about you?
3. What is good about being different from our peers?
4. Are you different, or do you tend to follow the crowd?
5. What may be bad about following a crowd?
6. How can you express your unique qualities in a positive manner?

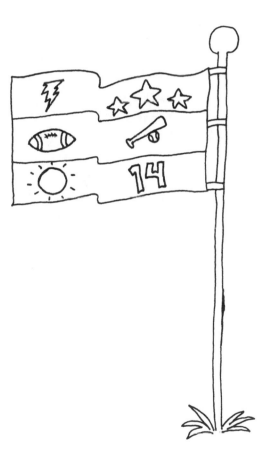

FREEZE

Being in front of a group of people and adapting quickly to a new situation takes quick thinking and the willingness to take a risk. Adapting to something different and out of the ordinary is very difficult for some people and can be a frightening experience. However, in order for someone to change the things that are happening in his/her own life, that person must take big risk and be able to adapt to new situations.

Objective
To learn about the importance of being able to adapt to a new situation, to be flexible and change if needed, and to be able to interact with others. To look at how different people like to be the center of attention while some shy away from it. To explore the art of drama as a interest to be pursued to increase self-esteem.

Who
People who have difficulty adapting to new situations and who need to learn to take risks if they are to take control of their own life and change it for the better.

Group Size
5 or more

Materials
➲ None

Description
This is a fun drama game that gets people to take risks and change a situation. Start with two people who stand up and are in front of the group on the "stage". The rest of the group is watching and in the "audience".

Give the two people in the front a scene, location or situation that they must act out. For example you may tell them they are fishing at a lake, and they must in their own way create this scene, act it out, dialog and do whatever they want with it. While they are acting it out they may change positions (i.e. they both are fishing, then they are both trying to reel in a really big fish together).

While the scene is being acted out the audience members should be looking for an opportunity to become involved in the drama by raising their hand and yelling "freeze" at anytime when they see a place that they want the scene to freeze. At this point the two people on the "stage" need to stop acting and pose in the position that they are in when they hear "freeze". For example if the two were reeling in a big fish together, they must be frozen in that position. The person who yells freeze then chooses whose place s/he wants to take and puts him/herself in that place and resumes the scene. S/he must then change the scene with dialog, and the other person must follows his/her lead to create a new scene that is then acted out. So, two people reeling in a fish may suddenly become two firemen with a big hose, a team playing tug-o-war, or two cowboys trying to rope a cow together. The scene goes on until the next person yells "freeze" and changes it.

NOTE: For younger kids it is sometimes a good idea to make them wait for ten seconds before yelling freeze because they are all so eager to get in the action.

Discussion Prompts

1. In this game, was it hard or easy for you to adapt to the different situations you were in?
2. Do you ever have trouble adapting to a situation?
3. Why is important to be able to change or adapt to a situation?
4. Did some people go up on the "stage" more than others did? Why?
5. Do you shy away from being the center of attention or do you like it? Why?
6. What did you learn about yourself as a result of this activity?
7. Does anyone have a interest in drama after doing this activity?

NEWSPAPER ABOUT ME

A newspaper tells the news like it is (or it's supposed to anyway). Writing a news piece about yourself may be difficult because it's hard to write objectively. This activity gives people the chance to write some stories about their own lives so they can share these stories with others. The best part is the stories can be as honest, opinionated or straightforward as the author wants them to be.

Objective
To create a personal newspaper and share with others about your own life, thoughts, and dreams.

Who
People who have trouble disclosing information about their life or who have difficulty sharing their feelings and thoughts with others.

Group Size
1 or more

Materials
- ➲ One copy of the following four pages per person
- ➲ Pens or pencils
- ➲ Colored markers, crayons or colored pencils

Description

Give everyone a copy of "Newspaper About Me" found on the next four pages (you may want to enlarge the pages to fit on a full size sheet of paper) and provide pens and/or pencils, colored markers, crayons or colored pencils. Allow time for everyone to fill in their own paper before having a sharing time in which people can share with the group (briefly or extensively) what they have created.

Discussion Prompts

Discuss each person's newspaper after they have shared it with the group.

Variation

➲ Create your own "Newspaper About Me" for people to fill in.

☆ News About Me ☆

Date

This is my life

About my Family

The best part about my life is...

HELP WANTED - *Jobs that I would apply for and like to do in my future*

Things I've learned that will help me in my future...

SPORTS SECTION

PERSONALS

I would make a
good friend
because:

_____

Friends
Wanted

MY PERSONAL PHOTO ALBUM

WiLL AWAY

When someone makes up a will, they think of their worldly possessions and decide to whom they want these items to go when they die. What if you could pass along your skills, knowledge and personality characteristics? Would it be easy to decide what you had that was worth giving away and who you would give these things to? Making a will based upon your own personality can be interesting and fun as you will see.

Objective
To explore the characteristics that each person in the group feels that they have that are positive. For people to think about the people in their lives and the different characteristics that they notice in them.

Who
People who have trouble recognizing what is unique and special about their own lives. People who need to think about the qualities their own friends and family have.

Group Size
1 or more

Materials
➲ Paper
➲ Pens or pencils

Description
Start the activity by explaining what a will is and how it is used, to ensure that a person's valuables are passed on to the important people in his/her life after death. Ask the group to think about the qualities and attributes that they have, that they feel are valuable, and to think about who it is that they would want to pass these traits on to if it were

possible. Pass out paper and pens or pencils and instruct the group that they are to draft a will stating their traits that they will be giving away and to whom each one will go.

For example...

"I give my soccer skills to Mary, a friend of mine who is on the varsity soccer team of her school. I give my Creativity to my friend Roberta because even though she is already creative she would love to be able to come up with more game ideas for her recreation therapy groups. To my neighbor who is a step-mom I give my good parenting skills that I was able to learn as I went along. To one of my family members I give my moral values because I think it may keep him/her out of trouble."

Allow enough time for people to think about this and write it down, then ask each person to share their will with the group. For added fun you may make an official looking seal or get a sticker to put on it when it has been completed.

Discussion Prompts

1. Was it easy or hard for you to think of attributes that you have that would be of value to others? Why?
2. What does your will say about you and the people that you know?
3. What trait does someone else have that you know that you would like to have passed on to you? Why?

GUESS THE FEELING

Some people expect you to guess how they are feeling, and they will tell you this after you have guessed wrong and after they expected you to act differently towards them. This can create problems in relationships and for people who may need emotional help from others. It isn't always easy to guess how someone is feeling especially in a society that expects everyone to be happy all the time.

Objective
To discover the importance of stating your feelings because if you expect others to guess how you are feeling but your feelings are not obvious then nobody will know what your needs are. To understand how we communicate with our body language and actions.

Who
People who have trouble sharing their feelings and emotions.

Group Size
6 to 20 is ideal

Materials
- ➲ Paper
- ➲ Pens or pencils

Description
Give each person in the group a small piece of paper and a pen or pencil. Select one person in the group, and ask this person to write down how s/he is feeling at the time (this must be done as a feeling word). Ask the rest of the group to try and guess how the selected person is feeling and to write down a feeling word on their paper as their guess and add their name on it.

The leader then collects all of the paper and mixes them up before reading them to the group. Read them once through so everyone can hear what all of the options are before they attempt to guess the one that was actually written by the selected person. As you read the papers through a second time, ask each person to vote for the one that s/he thinks was written by the selected individual. Give a point to anyone who guesses correctly. Give a bonus point to anyone who wrote down the correct feeling on his/her paper. Do this for each person in the group if possible.

Discussion Prompts

1. Who in the group was easiest to guess about how they were feeling? Who was the most difficult? Why?
2. Do you think others always know how you are feeling?
3. Do you hide your feelings from others? Why or why not?
4. Is there ever a time when it may be OK to hide your feelings? If so, when? If not, why?
5. When can showing and stating your feelings help you in your life?

SAYiNG SOMETHiNG NEW

Comic strips are fun to read, especially the Sunday comics. Have you ever tried to guess what the story is before reading the words of the strip by simply looking at the pictures? Sometimes it is obvious what they are saying by looking at the characters' reactions and expressions but other times it is not so easy. By changing the words to a comic strip, an old strip can become new and at the same time give people a way to look at body language and facial expressions and to relate these to the emotions a person is feeling.

Objective
For people to match body language with an emotion or feeling. To allow individuals the opportunity to express their feelings in an indirect, non-threatening manner.

Who
People who need to learn to read the body language of others and to learn to react appropriately to how a person is feeling.

Group Size
1 or more

Materials
- ➲ A variety of comic strips found in your local paper (preferably from Sunday)
- ➲ Paper
- ➲ Pens or pencils
- ➲ Scissors
- ➲ Glue

Description

Prior to the activity go through your local paper and cut out a variety of different comic strips. Try to select comics in which the characters appear to be expressing different emotions. Then take blank paper and cut out pieces to glue over the words so that they are covered.

Once you are ready to start the activity, give each person a different comic strip. Instruct the group that they are to look at the pictures and based upon what the characters are doing put words into their mouths by writing these words in the blank spaces of the strip. When the new strip is finished, the words should fit the pictures, and the comic should make sense and tell a story.

You may wish to allow people to select from the comic strips that you have provided. You may suggest that the story or what the characters are saying reflect how the person who added the words is feeling at the time.

Discussion Prompts

1. What do our expressions and body language say about us?
2. Do you find it difficult to express how you are feeling? Why or why not?
3. When is it important to be able to express how you are feeling?
4. Are you able to read the body language clues of others? Why or why not?
5. Why is it important to be able to read someone else's body language?

Variation

- Select one strip at a time to show to the group and ask each person to write down on a piece of paper the words that they would fill in for each strip.

FEELINGS SHOT

Using body language, actions and facial expressions is important when sharing feelings and emotions. Some people have difficulty stating what they feel and expect the people around them to read their body language while others say how they are feeling but these feelings don't always match their actions. Being able to communicate one's feelings and emotions verbally as well as through body language is important and a fun part of this game.

Objective
For people to show the ability to appropriately express their feelings and to be able to recognize what emotion is being expressed by others in the group.

Who
People who have difficulty expressing their feelings and emotions. People whose body language doesn't match how they say they are feeling. People who need to learn to recognize the feelings and emotions of others.

Group Size
3 or more

Materials
- ◗ Basketball
- ◗ Basketball hoop

Description
Select one member of the group at a time to secretly select a feeling or emotion (they may need a list to select from). Once the individual has chosen an emotion give him/her the basketball and instruct him/her to act out this feeling when dribbling the ball and shooting at the

basket. Allow the rest of the group to guess which emotion is being acted out and the one who guesses correctly gets to go next.

Discussion Prompts
1. Was it easy or hard for you to act out the different emotions? Why?
2. Do you show your emotions easily or hide them by acting out other emotions? Why?
3. When is it important to not hide your emotions? Why?

INTERVIEW

There are many shows on the TV or radio that interview people. Sometimes the person being interviewed is asked some hard questions and their answers are either defensive or surprisingly candid. When listening to an interview, you never know what will come up as shown in this activity. An "interview" can be a fun, nonthreatening way to get people to open up a little more.

Objective
For people to share about their families in a nonthreatening manner.

Who
People who have difficulty sharing about the dynamics, feelings and relations within their family and who could benefit from sharing these things with others.

Group Size
1 to 8 is ideal

Materials
➲ Tape recorder
➲ Blank tape

Description
Select one person to be interviewed in the group and set the tape recorder up so that it can be spoken into and voices recorded. Ask the person who will be interviewed to think of someone, such as a neighbor, family friend or relative, who knows his/her family well. Instruct the person that s/he is to be that person for the activity. Now the leader and/or the members of the group will interview this person and ask questions about his/her family and the person being interviewed must answer in character.

The interviewer/s may ask "So, neighbor Bob what do your neighbors do for fun?"; and the person being interviewed would answer as if s/he were neighbor Bob about the real person's own family. The tape player is for added fun and to make the activity less threatening (or more so for some people). The tape may be played back or simply taped over for the next person or kept for a later session.

You may have prepared questions or ad lib. You may allow different group members to ask questions so that they will be involved or just allow the leader to ask the questions. The interview may be done individually or in a small group.

Discussion Prompts

Discussion takes place during the activity itself or play the tape back and allow people to stop the tape and to ask questions at this time.

IMPRESSIONS RELAY

Stating how you feel when you are directly asked can be difficult. Some people who don't want others to know their true feelings may lie or hide the truth when asked. However, if one is asked anonymously or in an indirect manner as in this game, telling the truth can become easier and even a bit less threatening.

Objective
For people to express how they are feeling in a nonthreatening manner and for them to get to know others in the group.

Who
People who have trouble expressing their feelings and emotions.

Group Size
8 or more

Materials
(For each team of 4 or more):
- ➲ 1 dry erase board with marker
- ➲ or chalkboard with chalk
- ➲ or sidewalk with sidewalk chalk
- ➲ or large sheet of paper with marker or crayon

Description
Divide the group into at least two teams of four or more. Line the teams up on one side of a room or play area with a writing surface and marker opposite each team on the other side of the play area. On the signal "go" the first person from each team must run to the writing

surface and write down a word that describes how s/he is feeling, then run back to his/her line, and the next person does the same. Encourage the group to be thoughtful and truthful when thinking of how they are feeling and to write the words in a random order on the board rather than in order of the people writing the words.

For large groups have everyone go through the line once, but for smaller group ask each person to go through the line more than once and to write down a different word each time.

A winner is declared when the first team finishes, but allow the other teams to continue so everyone gets equal chances to write down their feelings. Now gather the group together and ask people to guess who wrote what and to discuss why they wrote what they did.

Discussion Prompts
1. Why did you write down the word/s that you did?
2. Do you feel that everyone in the group was being honest about how they were feeling? Why or why not?
3. Do you have trouble expressing how you feel verbally?
4. Is it easier for anyone in the group to express their feelings on paper than verbally? Why?
5. What did you learn about others in the group today?

BE A BiKE

What would the everyday items that you use say about you if they could talk? Maybe these items would tell a story that would surprise and amaze those who think they know you best. Or these items could give a great deal of information to someone who was trying to get to know you.

Objective
To talk about yourself to others in a fun, descriptive, detailed, yet nonthreatening manner. To promote group bonding through discussion and sharing.

Who
People who have difficulty talking about themselves and sharing about their own lives but who could benefit from doing so.

Group Size
2 to 10 is ideal

Materials
➲ None

Description
Gather the group together and ask people to take turns answering the question "if your bike could talk what would it say about you?" Do several rounds of this and replace the word bike with different objects that people come in contact with frequently.
Some ideas are…
Bike, Coat, Spoon, TV, Phone, Stereo, Pencil, Schoolbook, Refrigerator, House, Toys, Shoes, Car, Computer, etc.

Discussion Prompts

Allow group members to ask questions about the answers given and hold a group discussion about any unusual or interesting answers.

PUPPET OF EMOTIONS

Being able to express emotions doesn't come easy for everyone. Some people are like puppets and tell you what they think you want them to say rather than express the true emotions they are feeling.

Objective

To encourage people to express their emotions and for them to identify the proper emotions to go with any given situation.

Who

People who have difficulty sharing their emotions.
People who have trouble identifying appropriate emotions to go with appropriate situations.

Group Size

1 or more

Materials

- ⊃ Paper lunch sacks (one per person)
- ⊃ Colored markers or crayons
- ⊃ Optional: Yarn, glitter, construction paper, ribbon, fabric, scissors, glue, etc.

Description

Give each person a paper bag to use to create a puppet, and supply the group with any materials you have available to decorate and personalize the puppets. Have them create their puppets by putting their hand into the bag and manipulating one side (the flap) of the bottom of the bag to form a mouth.

Select an emotion that you would like each puppet to be expressing (may be the same for everyone or give each person his/her own emotion). For example you may ask a group member to create a puppet that is "angry" by using the supplies available to make the face and other features.

Once everyone has created his/her puppet, allow time for sharing, then have them do any of the following: (some require that the puppets have different emotions).

1. Have each person write on the back of his/her puppet the things that a person who feels that emotion might say or do.
2. Have people write down things on their own puppets that make them feel the emotion that is being expressed.
3. Ask the group to get together and create a puppet show with each puppet in it expressing the assigned emotion as a part of the story line.
4. Create situations that are open-ended and ask each person how his/her puppet would respond to the situation.
5. Ask people to state how they are feeling using the appropriate puppet.
6. Use your imagination and be creative!!

Discussion Prompts

1. What emotion is most difficult for you to express and why?
2. What emotion do you most often feel and why?
3. What did you learn about yourself as a result of this activity?

BiG WiND BLOWS

One of the biggest risk people can take in life is to open up to others and share their thoughts, feelings, struggles and pains. However, when the risk taking starts out non-threatening and then deepens in the course of a fun game, as it does in Big Wind Blows, people begin to open up and take risk without even realizing they are doing so.

Objective
To explore what we have in common with others and what our differences are. For a group of people to increase their level of risk taking in order to help individual's open up and be more comfortable with each other.

Who
People who need to become more comfortable with the group they are with so they can open up and take risk when sharing.

Group Size
6 or more (more is better!!)

Materials
➲   Small pieces of scrap paper (about 3inches by 3inches is good)

Description
Gather the group into a circle and give each person a piece of paper and instruct everyone to stand on their piece of paper. The leader starts in the middle of the circle. The leader doesn't want to be in the middle (or "it") but rather on one of the spots so his/her job is to make people move off of their spots so s/he can get out of being in the middle.

The person in the middle must say something that is true about his/her own life. For example, a person who likes to play soccer might say "The big wind blows for everyone who likes soccer" and everyone who likes soccer must move from their spot and find another empty spot to stand on. There will always be one less spot than there are people so a new person will end up in the middle after each round. Tell everyone that once they leave their spot they must find another spot and may not return to their own, in that turn.

After playing "The Big Wind Blows" for a few rounds add the following changes to make it more challenging, revealing and to build the risk-taking factor of the group. Keep changing it throughout the game and build up to increased risk taking. The person in the middle must fill in the ( ) with something related to the subject that is applicable to his/her life.

The Big Wind Blows for (something you like about yourself)
The Big Wind Blows for (something you want to do with your future)
The Big Wind Blows for (something you are afraid of)
The Big Wind Blows for (something nobody knows about you)
The Big Wind Blows for (something that makes you sad or angry)
The Big Wind Blows for (what you do when you become angry)
The Big Wind Blows for (challenge the group to take a risk)

When challenging the group to take a risk it seems that the bigger the risk taken by the first person, the more willing people are to open up and take a risk themselves. Remember that it should be a "challenge" and not something people have to do.

If the leader goes first for the risk taking one then the deepness of their risk may dictate the amount of risk taking the group takes during the game. Giving examples also helps people out. Here are some of the bigger risks that have been taken during this game to give you ideas: The Big wind blows for... "anyone who has lost a family member", "been through a divorce", "used drugs", "has acne", "battles a weight problem", and "anyone who has been depressed in the last week". Remind people that it can be a risk to run as well as to be in the middle and challenge people to be honest.

Discussion Prompts

1. What did you notice about yourself as a result of this game? (more questions found on the next page)

2. Were you ever afraid to admit that you related to what was said? Why?
3. Did you find out that you have more differences, or more similarities with others? How do you feel about this?
4. Why is it good to find out who else has been through the same thing that we have been through?
5. Did you learn anything interesting about someone else in the group that you didn't know before? Is so, what?
6. Was it easy or hard for you to take a risk? Why?
7. What is a risk that you want to take to change your life?
8. What keeps you from taking risk?
9. What kinds of risk can be helpful for you?

Variation
➲ People may sit for the game in chairs or lay hula-hoops on the ground that people must stand in, rather than having people stand on a piece of paper on the floor.

MORE FAMILY SCULPTURES

Family sculptures are popular in therapy and give the therapist a window to look through to see the family dynamics, relations and situations that are going on with each person. You can find the activity of family sculpture in the book *The wRECking Yard*. It is a simple activity in which an individual uses group members as props to "sculpt" into his/her own family by placing these people in poses and specific distances from each other in order to create a sculpture that represents his/her own family dynamics. The sculpture that is created allows others to take a look at each family and to learn more about the person who created it.

After traveling around the country giving workshops, I have discovered a wide variety of variations to this one simple activity that are well worth passing along. Family sculptures seem to be popular with therapist and counselors and hopefully you will gain more worthwhile ideas from the variations here!

Objective
To provide a non-threatening setting for people to share their family dynamics with the rest of the group. To open the door for future discussions concerning family relationships.

Who
People who have difficulty talking about their families.

Group Size
6 or more is ideal but for some of the sculpture variations the group may be as small as one person.

Materials
None to varied (depending on the activity chosen)

Description

In addition to the family sculpture activity found in *The wRECking Yard* here are some variations to the old theme of creating a sculpture of your family. Remember a family can be biological, foster, a group home or whoever each person feels is their family.

OBJECT SCULPTURE: Use objects such as crayons, candy, playing cards, pencils or whatever else is handy for the sculptures. People then place the objects on the table a certain distance or closeness to each other to represent their family relations. If using something like crayons they may pick different colors to represent how they see various family members.

ANIMAL FAMILY: Collect a wide variety of stuffed animals and give people the choice of what animal will represent each family member and the opportunity to place the animals in a "sculpture" that is representative of the relations between family members.

HOLIDAY SCULPTURE: Each person creates a sculpture of his/her family as they would be during a specific holiday. A sculpture may be the family sitting around the thanksgiving table, around the Christmas tree, at Easter, a birthday party etc.

FAMILY CIRCUS: Select different circus performers, characters, or anyone related to a circus to be used to represent different family members and their relationships with one another.

FAMILY CLOCK: Sculpt a family at different times of the day: in the morning, the daytime, and at dinner.

SPEAKING SCUPLPTURE: Each person makes a family sculpture of his/her family; then s/he goes around to each person in the sculpture and says whatever it is that s/he would like to say to that "family member". Encourage people to say something that may be difficult to say, such as "thank you" or "I feel hurt because...".

EMOTION SCULPTURE: Set the stage for the family sculpture at the beginning of the activity by stating an emotion such as anger. Each person must then pose his/her family as they would be in relation to each other when dealing with that emotion, feeling, or situation.

IDEAL FAMILY: Each person creates their idea of what an ideal family would be. This sculpture doesn't have to be made up of the people that are in their family but rather what they view as the "ideal" family.

THE FAMILY - FAMILY SCULPTURE: If you work with families in counseling settings, ask each family member to pose their family as they see them in relationship to each other. For example if the dad is always working and never home, he may be placed at work rather than in the home with the rest of the family.

BEFORE AND AFTER: Ask people to make a family sculpture of how their family was before a situation and then to make another sculpture of how they think their family is now, after the event. Examples are: before and after a divorce, a death, birth, move or any other major family event.

GROUP SCULPTURE: If you are working with a group of people, ask different people in the group to make a sculpture of how they see the group. Place people together based on who in the group is friends with whom and who may be left out etc. Ask more than one person to make a sculpture of the same group so the perceived differences can be seen.

Discussion Prompts
Discuss each sculpture after it is created. Allow the "artist" to explain his/her sculpture and for others to ask questions.

WHAT'S YOUR GPA?

When you are in school, a report card is very important and eagerly awaited (or dreaded) at the end of each semester. Grades given out by teachers are usually based upon performance but sometimes they are based upon the teacher's opinion of how well the person actually did. At the end of each report card there is the GPA (Grade Point Average) which may determine where a person goes to college or what job they get after high school.

What if each person evaluated him/herself instead of the teachers giving out the grades? Would some people have higher grades than usual and some have lower? What if the grades were based on your ability to be a good person and to get along with others, rather than on academic performance?

This is a fun way to determine what grades people would give themselves if given the chance and to see what standards each person has for his/her own life.

Objective
To take responsibility for your own behavior and recognize areas that could use improvement.

Who
People who need to take responsibility for their own actions and who need to take steps towards changing their own lives for the better.

Group Size
1 or more

Materials
- 1 copy of "My Report Card" per person
- Pens or pencils

Description

Give each person a copy of "My Report Card" (found on the following page) and a pen or pencil. Instruct them to grade themselves in each of the listed areas using the standard A,B,C,D,F grading scale and to give comments as to ways that they could improve each behavior, if needed, or compliments if more appropriate to the grade given. The grade should be based upon a self-evaluation by each person of his/her own life. After everyone has completed the activity challenge each person to share his/her report card with the group.

Discussion Prompts

1. Do you feel you were hard, easy or fair on yourself? Why?
2. Do you feel that someone else in the group was too hard on themselves or too easy? Who and why?
3. If you recognize the areas that you need improvement in, are you taking steps towards improving yourself? Why or why not?
4. What can you do to change your grades?
5. Are you willing to work on getting better grades? Why or why not?

MY REPORT CARD

Listening to others _____
Comments:

Sharing with others _____
Comments:

My manners _____
Comments:

Following directions _____
Comments:

Anger management _____
Comments:

Stating my feelings clearly _____
Comments:

Helping others _____
Comments:

Accepting help from others _____
Comments:

ANGER
MANAGEMENT

Anger is a powerful emotion that can often get people into trouble, and spending time working in a psychiatric hospital makes this all too clear. A boy who sets a church on fire, a girl who throws a brick through the window of her parents' home, and the many other people who cause harm to themselves or to others and who must spend time in counseling are all examples of anger getting out of control. Anger is a difficult issue to address, and it takes a long time for people to work through deep feelings that have been building for years. Fortunately games can be a powerful tool when used as a part of an anger management program to help people understand their behavior.

Creating games that help people address their anger is a difficult and challenging task. When using games in other therapeutic domains such as communication, and teamwork, people practice using these skills during the course of the game itself. With anger it is possible to have people practice using anger control during a game if the game leads them to become frustrated and angry as they might in a competitive game (this is discussed further in *The wRECking Yard*). On the other hand an anger management game may simply allow people to discuss what it is they might do when in a situation that makes them angry, in hopes that they will use these coping skills when the time comes. Discussion activities are fine and serve a purpose but in order for games to have a strong therapeutic impact, being involved in an experience is more powerful than being involved in a discussion. This is especially true for anger management activities and this is why it is so challenging to create good effective games that address anger.

People's anger comes in many different forms but the two that are most easily addressed and that are focused on in the games of this book are "acting out" anger and "deep down hidden" anger. People who let out their anger in an overly aggressive manner that causes harm or damage to property, themselves, or others are in the category of acting out anger. On the other hand those who keep their pain and anger hidden deep down inside until it becomes self-destructive are in the class of deep down hidden anger. Acting out anger is more easily addressed because it is visible, especially in a game that is unfair, frustrating, competitive or that makes a person angry.

The games in this chapter address both kinds of anger in different games. The games are meant to be experiential and interactive with strong lessons that open doors for discussion.

ANGER
MANAGEMENT
GAMES AND
ACTIVITIES

MOVING ON

Some people have things in their lives that make them very angry, upset, and hurt. These things keep them from moving on with a healthy and happy life. It is important for people to let go of the anger as much as they can so it doesn't eat at them on the inside. Part of letting go of any anger is first realizing what causes the anger, then sharing this feeling with others, and in this activity, releasing it in a symbolic manner.

Objective

For people to express their anger in an appropriate manner towards something or someone who has hurt them.
For people to map out a positive path that they can follow in their lives once they have released their anger.

Who

People who harbor anger inside and have difficulty releasing it.
People who have difficulty releasing anger in an appropriate manner.
People who have anger towards something or someone and who are unable to see a positive future ahead because of all the anger held inside.

Group Size

1 or more

Materials

- A "Hot Wheels®" race track
- Several small cars that can run on the racetrack
- A cardboard picture frame or small box
- Newsprint paper
- Colored markers or crayons
- Tape

Description

Prior to the activity set up the racetrack so that it goes from a high point (i.e. the edge of a chair or a table) to a jump, with the picture frame (or box) set up at the end of the jump. A car should be able to race down the track, go off the jump into the air and through the picture frame.

Ask each person in the group to think of something or someone that they feel anger towards. Each person should express their anger towards something appropriate (i.e. "I'm mad because I've been abused" or "I'm angry because I have a mental illness and it's not fair"; an inappropriate response would be "I'm mad at my teacher because she always gives me a time out"). Then allow time for everyone to draw a picture of the person or thing that makes them angry.

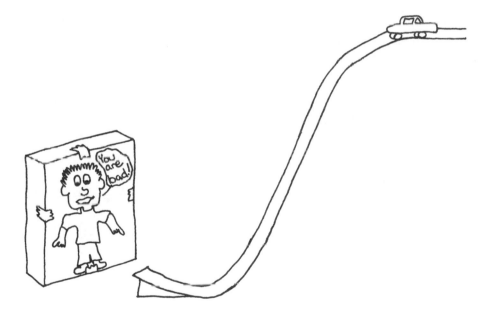

Once everyone has drawn their picture, ask everyone to gather around the racetrack that you have set up. Explain to the group that they will each get a turn to "smash through" the anger that they are feeling and then get the opportunity to move on with their lives in a positive way. Each person then takes their turn taping their picture into the picture frame, telling the group what it is that makes them angry and then choosing a car that they want to run down the track. Once a car is chosen the individual runs it down the track and watches as it jumps through the picture. Have a ceremonial throw away box where they may discard their picture after their turn.

It is a good idea to test your track with the paper you are using prior to doing this activity to make sure it will break when a car goes through it.

After everyone has taken a turn at the racetrack, gather the group together for the second half of the activity. Ask each person to draw the road that their car will be traveling down now that they have released their anger. Along the road there should be some places to stop when they need support and some places they can go where they feel happy, safe and anger free. Encourage the group to be creative and to make a travel plan that is positive and happy rather than one that is angry and bitter. This is one of those activities where it may be best to create a sample map before hand to show the group.

Once everyone has completed their map allow time for sharing and discussion.

Discussion Prompts
1. How did you feel when you were drawing your picture?
2. How did you feel when your car went through the picture?
3. What happens when we keep anger inside and do not release it?
4. What are some other ways to release anger? Are they good or bad ways?
5. Is your road different than it would have been if you hadn't run your car through the thing that was making you angry?
6. How do you feel after doing this activity?

HiDDEN HEART

The things that we keep hidden inside are our hurts, emotional pain, scars, and anger. Some people work extra hard to hide these feelings and eventually may physically hurt themselves or others if they don't share their feelings with others.

This activity gives people the opportunity to share their pain and the anger they have hidden inside. When people start to deal with these feelings of anger before becoming destructive they can experience happiness in their lives once again.

Objective
For people to recognize and understand that the anger they keep on the inside affects how they live their lives. To help people recognize the good things that they have in their hearts and to encourage them to share this part of themselves with others.

Who
People who are angry about their own lives and who show this anger easily to others. People who are angry on the inside and keep the anger buried deep down which leads them to have many negative feelings towards themselves or towards others.

Group Size
1 or more

Materials
- Paper
- Pens or pencils
- Scissors
- Thin pieces of ribbon
- One small, and one large balloon for each person (not inflated)
- Permanent colored markers

Description

Give each person a small balloon, piece of ribbon, paper, scissors and a pen or pencil. Explain to them that this balloon represents their heart and all of the pain, hurt and anger that can be found inside of it. Instruct them to cut slips of paper that are small enough to fit into the balloon, to write down their hurts and anger on these, and to then put the papers into the balloon and tie the balloon closed with the ribbon (do not blow up the balloon). These papers do not have to be shown to anyone.

Give each person one of the larger balloons and ask each person to put their "heart" (the smaller balloon) into the larger balloon. Instruct each person to blow up the large balloon and tie it shut. Tell them that they are to write on the outside of the balloon how they present themselves to others on the outside so that nobody can see the things that are hidden on the inside. Some people use humor to hide the pain; others always act confident even though they feel insecure and lonely. These are the types of things people should write on the outside of their balloon.

Once all of the balloons are written on, gather the group together and discuss what is written on the outside of the balloons. Challenge the members of the group to each share at least one thing they have written down on the outside of their balloon. Then ask each person to state if it is a good thing to cover up what is on the inside or if they would like people to know more about what's going on in their life and if so to think of a way that this can happen. After this discussion, allow them to pop their balloons as a symbolic way of getting rid of all the walls and devices that they use to hide their pain.

After the balloons are popped, the hearts with the ribbons tied around them should remain. Challenge each person in the group to find someone in the next week's time whom they trust enough to give their heart to. They should explain to that person what the balloon represents and why they want to give it to them; they should then let that person untie the ribbon to see what is inside. If possible bring the group back together a week later for a follow up group to find out who was able to find someone to give their heart to. Or simply challenge the group to read what they had in their "heart" to the group.

Discussion Prompts

1. How are you affected by the feelings and emotions that you keep inside of you?
2. What things inside of you makes you feel angry?
3. How can your life change if you get rid of the negative things and leave only the positive in your heart?
4. How can you get rid of the negative things in your life?
5. Do you trust anyone with your heart? Why or why not?
6. How can it help you to find someone to trust with your feelings and emotions?

Variation

➲ Simply place a piece of paper with your name on it inside a balloon to represent you as a person and then write down the things that you do to keep people from getting to know the "real" you on the outside and share these with the group.

OUT OF CONTROL

Many people want to control every aspect of their lives and when things feel out of control or someone else is setting the rules that they must live by, they become frustrated and angry. Some people have difficulty controlling this anger and need to learn how to accept the things in their lives that seem out of control.

Objective
For people to realize that they cannot control everything in their lives and that they must learn how to deal with things that seem out of control, rather than giving in to anger and frustration.

Who
People who become easily angered or frustrated when things don't go the way they want them to or in their favor.

Group Size
4 to 15

Materials
- Several small prizes (any items the group members would like) wrapped in wrapping paper
- One pair of dice

Description
Prior to the activity gather together some small prize items and wrap them. There should be at least one prize for each participant plus a few extra. Place all of the prizes on a table and gather the group around.

Instruct the group that the game will be played in two different parts (do not explain the second part until the first part is completed). In the first round of the game one person starts with a pair of dice and rolls them once. If s/he rolls a double, s/he may select a prize from the pile, unwrap it and set it on the table in front of him/her for the rest of the group to see. If a double is not rolled, the dice are passed to the next person who attempts to roll a double in order to get a prize. Everyone in the group continues to roll and pass the dice (collecting prizes for a double) until all of the prizes in the middle are gone. In the end one person may end up with two or three prizes while others may end up with nothing.

Introduce the second part of the game at this point. This half is timed (for a smaller group use about five minutes and about ten minutes for a larger group). The game is played in the same manner as it was for the first part only now instead of selecting a prize from the middle when a double is rolled, a prize may be selected from anyone else in the group. This continues until the allotted time is up. Again, some people may end up with more prizes in front of them than others.

This is a fun, high-energy activity; be prepared for the group to get a bit loud with excitement.

Discussion Prompts
1. What do you do when "the luck of the roll" does not always go your way?
2. Do you feel like you have control over your life?
3. How do you handle things when life feels out of control or unfair?
4. Does anyone feel angry about this game? If so, how have you handled this feeling?
5. What can you do when life feels unfair and things do not go your way?

Variation
➲ Candy bars may be used in place of prizes and do not need to be wrapped in wrapping paper but should be left in the candy bar wrapping.

THE UNFAiR GAME

Sometimes life can really seem unfair! For some unfortunate people, life may seem even more unfair than for others.

This game is unfair, but don't tell that to those who are playing until it is all over because who would want to play a game if they knew the leader had set it up so s/he would win.

When the game is unfair, people may not get angry, but in real life many people who feel their life is unfair or who have trouble following the rules will have a lot to talk about at the end of this game.

The Unfair Game is another one of the favorites at the Therapeutic Activities and Games workshops and has been used by many of the people who have learned it as a part of varying diverse anger management programs.

Objective
For individuals to practice using anger control when in a situation that is clearly unfair and frustrating.

Who
People who have difficulty controlling their anger.
People who become easily frustrated when a situation does not go in their favor.

Group Size
3 to 15 Participants

Materials
- Deck of Cards
- Pair of dice
- Bag of candy (each piece should be individually wrapped) - about 5 pieces per person
- Copies of the rules (found on the following pages)

Description

It is important to read ALL the directions to this game prior to playing it with your group.

Prior to the activity take all but a couple of the spades out of the deck of cards and mix the few spades left towards the top of the deck. If possible have two identical decks of cards and replace the spades with cards from a different suit from the spare deck.

Start by gathering the group into a circle and by giving everyone five pieces of candy. Inform the group that they will be able to keep whatever candy they have at the end of the game (and candy may not be eaten until the end). Have a few copies of the rules out on the table for players to refer to during the game (found on the following two pages; you may want to read them before continuing on). It is also important that you - the leader - participate in the game.

Either set a time limit or end the game when a few people are eliminated or when the pot is filled with a bunch of candy. At the end of the time limit select the person with the best sportsmanship. Of course this person is you - the leader - (since this *is* the Unfair Game), so you select yourself and take all the candy left in the middle.

The idea is to make sure that this game is truly unfair, just as life can often be. It is often our tendency to pass out candy to everyone at the close of a game like this. Resist this temptation in order for the game to have a stronger effect. Keep it for a later day or another game! To heighten the effect you may wish to reveal the truth about the deck of cards if they don't figure out that the deck is stacked against them.

Also don't tell them that this is called "The Unfair Game" until the end; just call it the "Candy Game" or something else so they don't catch on until the game is over.

Discussion Prompts

1. Was this game unfair? Why or why not?
2. How do you feel right now?
3. Do you ever feel like your life is unfair? If so, when and how do you handle it when things seem unfair?
4. Do you think it would help you in your own life to change how you act when life seems unfair? If so, how?

Rules of the Game

1. When it is your turn you may roll the dice or select a card

2. If you roll the dice and get:

~ <u>Odd</u> - you must put a piece of candy in the "pot" (a place in the middle of the table)

~ <u>Even</u> - you may take a piece of candy from anyone else's pile

~ <u>Double</u> - you must give a piece of candy to someone else in the group (this does not count as an even number)

3. If you draw a card and get:

~ <u>Heart</u> - you must give a piece of candy to the person on your right

~ <u>Club</u> - you must give a piece of candy to the person on your left

~ <u>Diamond</u> - you must put a piece of candy in the pot

~ <u>Spade</u> - you get two pieces of candy from the pot (or from a person/s of your choice if the pot is empty)

4. If anyone is unfortunate enough to lose all of their candy, they are then eliminated from the game.

5. If you are eliminated from the game you may continue to sit in the circle but can return to the game only if someone gives you a piece of candy during the course of the game (no candy may be given to an eliminated person out of the goodness of your heart; it must be determined by the cards or dice).

6. The leader decides who displayed the best sportsmanship during the game, and this person gets to keep all the candy left in the pot at the end of the game.

7. After an allotted time the person who has the most candy wins, and everyone may keep any candy they have acquired.

BiG VS. SMALL

Being put into an unfair situation isn't fun for anyone; and some people who lack anger control will act out in this type of situation. This game is a good object lesson in how things can (at times) be unfair, unbalanced, or mismatched. This game is also a good discussion starter in what is unfair in people's lives and how it should be handled, especially for those who are easily angered and who become destructive when things don't go their way.

Objective
For individuals to practice using anger control when in a situation that is clearly unfair and frustrating.

Who
People who have difficulty controlling their anger.
People who become easily frustrated when a situation does not go in their favor.

Group Size
4 or more

Materials
➲ A basketball, volleyball or beach ball

Description
Ask the group to line up from shortest to tallest. Divide the line in half so all the short people are on one team and all the tall people are on the other. Set up a game for the group to play in which height is an advantage. Some suggestions are: basketball, volleyball or keep away with a beach ball.

After playing this way for a while, the tall team will most likely be winning with the short team being a bit frustrated. At this point change the rules and tell the tall team that they must all put one hand in their pocket or behind their backs for the rest of the game.

Discussion Prompts

1. How did you feel when the game was in your favor?
2. How did you feel when the game was not in your favor?
3. Do you ever feel like your life is like this game? Are you usually winning or losing?
4. Do you ever get angry when things seem to be unfair?
5. How do you release the anger that you feel when things are unfair?
6. Is there a better way to handle an unfair situation?

BODY OF ANGER

As you become angry your body begin to show signs of our anger. For each person the signs are different, but often very similar. Your heart beats faster; you become anxious, have rapid breathing, begin to sweat, etc. The key to controlling anger is recognizing that you are becoming angry so you can act responsibly rather than reacting to the feeling irresponsibly after it is too late.

Objective
To discuss and learn how our bodies react when we become angry so that individuals can detect the signs of anger and take measures to begin to control their anger before they become out of control.

Who
People who need to learn to recognize when their bodies are showing signs of becoming angry so they can use their anger control skills before they act out.

Group Size
2 or more

Materials
- An old white T-shirt that can be written on
- An old pair of pants that can be written on (or shorts and body paint)
- Face paint
- Markers that can be used on fabric

Description
Ask for a volunteer to put on the old clothes that you have gathered and ask him/her to stand in front of the group. The leader then asks the group to think of all the distinct ways their bodies react when they feel

angry. As people name different things, have someone write them down on the part of the body with face paint or on the clothes with markers where they apply. (This should be kept appropriate and works best on a male volunteer). For example, "rapid breathing" could be written on the chest to represent the lungs, "red face" on a cheek to represent face turning red and all the other unique traits of anger that the group comes up with.

This may be done with a large group or in smaller groups who share what they have created with the rest of the group when the activity is finished.

Discussion Prompts
1. Which body reaction do you most identify with?
2. How do you control your anger?
3. How do you release feelings of tension?
4. Why do you think our bodies react like they do to anger?
5. How can you use your body signals to help you control your anger?

Variation
➲ Trace someone in the group on paper and use his/her body tracing to create a "body of anger" on.

GOOD, BAD AND UGLY

There are many ways of expressing anger. Some ways are ugly –
such as starting a fight, taking drugs, or vandalizing property. Bad ways
of handling anger are overeating, spending too much money, or similar
indulgences. Good ways of controlling anger are taking a self-timeout,
talking to someone about your feelings, or writing in a journal.

This activity is about learning the good ways of dealing with anger
and getting rid of the bad and the ugly ways.

Objective
To determine positive ways of handling anger as opposed to the
negative ways that individuals are currently using to cope with anger.
To promote discussion of different ways to handle anger and discuss
the effect these actions have on people's lives.

Who
People who express their anger in a way that is dangerous to
themselves, dangerous to others, or destructive to property.

Group Size
1 or more

Materials
- ➲ 3x5 cards or small pieces of paper
- ➲ Pens or pencils
- ➲ 3 small boxes

Description
Give each person in the group a pile of 3x5 cards or small pieces of
paper and a pen or pencil. Ask them to create three piles in front of
them and to write "Good" on the top of the card in one pile, "Bad" on
another and "Ugly" on the third.

Create a few scenarios that would likely make the people in your group angry based upon what you know about them and read these to the group one at time. Or, ask individual group members to share a time when they became really angry and to describe the scene.

After a scenario is read each person must write down a good way of handling the situation on the "good" card, a bad way on the "bad" card and an ugly way on the "ugly" card. Have three boxes labeled good, bad and ugly ready and ask people to put their cards in the respective boxes when finished. Do this for several different situation scenarios.

After all the situations have been stated or read and all the cards have been turned in, take the ugly box and read the cards, one at a time. After each card ask people to raise their hands if they have ever expressed their anger in this manner and to state what happened, also discuss the consequences or benefits of handling anger in this manner. Do this next for the bad box and conclude with the good box.

Discussion Prompts

1. What did you learn as a result of this activity?
2. Do you tend to express your anger in a good, bad or ugly manner most often? Why?
3. Which way works best for you? Is this a good way?
4. What would be the best way for you to handle your anger?

MAD MUSIC

Spending a day watching the news, reading the newspapers, or listening to music that has a negative message can really bring you down. If you instead choose to spend the day surrounded with positive things, people, news and music, your attitude and outlook on life can change dramatically.

The problem is that many people are not even aware of the amount of negative things that they see and hear in one day and don't realize the effect such influences can have on their lives and how it can make them more angry than they may already be.

Objective
To explore feelings that different people have when angry and explore how music can affect these feelings.

Who
People who surround themselves with negative influences and who don't recognize the impact that these influences can have on their lives.

Group Size
1 or more

Materials
- A stereo, tape player or compact disk player
- A selection of Rock and Roll or Rap music that has a negative message (or any kind of music that is negative)
- Paper
- Pens or pencils

Description
Prior to this activity gather together a selection of songs that have a negative message or story in them.

Gather the group together and simply explain to the group that they will be listening to different songs and that you want them to draw a picture of what the song is about, of what the person singing the song must look like, or how they are feeling while listening to the music. Do not inform the group that the songs are all about negative topics. After listening to all the music, allow time for each person to share the feelings that they had written down on their paper before asking the group the discussion questions.

Discussion Prompts

1. If any of this music made you feel good, why do you think this is?
2. Do you gravitate towards things that are negative? Why or why not?
3. If this music made you feel negative, why do you think that was?
4. Can your environment affect how you feel?
5. What kind of environment are you in?
6. How can you change the negative things you are surrounded by into positive things?
7. How can your simple choice of music affect your life?
8. Do you think that you need to change the type of music that you listen to? Why or why not? What would you like to change it to?

Variation

➲ Ask people to bring music that they feel is negative and a selection of music that they think is positive, then compare the two.

COPiNG SKiLLS

"Just say no" is a popular slogan that is used today as a way of giving kids a coping skill to use against the pressures of today's society. It is meant to send the message to young people that they have a choice of whether or not they drink, do drugs or participate in any other activities that are self-destructive. This message is pounded into the heads of young people from the time they are very young and they continue hearing it on into adulthood. This message makes sense and seems to have good intentions, but perhaps what community leaders, teachers, counselors and parents should be teaching the young people of today's society is "just say yes".

Just as youth should be given the power to say "no" to negative influences and choices, they can use this same power to say "yes" to positive options that are given to them. What are the positive and healthy things that they can say "yes" to? As teachers, counselors, leaders and parents, it is our job to present youth with these positive options. Rather than always focusing on what they shouldn't do, we should give them a wide variety of choices of things that they can do to build self-esteem, promote healthy friendships, have fun, and that offer a future of hope.

Games and activities are powerful tools to be used when focusing on "yes" rather than focusing on "no". Many people are stuck in a lifestyle that is negative because they don't know what else there is to do with their free time. Finding new games and activities to engage in isn't always an easy task, but with the help of others there are many doors that can be opened and numerous new coping skills that can be gathered for a person to use in his/her life.

The first step in helping people gain new coping skills is to help make them aware of how they currently cope with difficulties and to then help them evaluate if these activities are emotionally, spiritually, and physically healthy for them to be engaged in. The next step is to introduce them to a wide variety of activities, options, resources and connections that can become healthy "yes" options. The final and the hardest step is to get them motivated to incorporate these new healthy options into theirs lives so they can use these activities as appropriate coping skills for the difficult things they face each day. The games and activities of this book cover the first two steps but the third step is up to the individual who needs to change. By offering encouragement and a wide spectrum of coping skills from which to choose a good leader can make a difference in how much effort and energy a person will be willing to put into saying "yes" to the good, while at the same time saying "no" to the bad.

COPING SKILLS GAMES AND ACTIVITIES

100

In the book *The wRECking Yard of games and activities* we talked about the benefits of both physical and mental exercise for everyone. By asking people how they feel physically and emotionally prior to an activity and then again after exercising, we can help them recognize the positive effects physical activity can have on their lives.

This game is a fun way for people to experience exercise and learn about the positive effects it can have on them at the same time.

Objective

To encourage people to engage in exercise to improve their own mental and physical health and to promote fitness as a coping skill.

Who

People who could benefit from exercising and who need to improve the amount of physical activity they engage in daily.
People who could benefit from learning about the effects exercise can have on them mentally.

Group Size

3 to 10 participants

Materials

- ➲ Basketball
- ➲ Basketball hoop
- ➲ Jump rope

Description

Challenge the group to work together to earn one hundred points by completing various fitness activities. Emphasize that this is not a competition but a challenge and everyone should do their best to support the group. Points can be earned by completing the following

activities (or create your own).
⇨ 1 point for each lap run in one minute
⇨ 1 point for each basket made (everyone gets 10 shots)
⇨ 1 point for each foot jumped in a standing long jump
⇨ 1 point for every five jumps made when jump roping without making a mistake (give each person 3 tries)
⇨ 1 point for each push up
⇨ 1 point for every 10 jumping jacks
Keep track of the points on paper and continually challenge the group to make it all the way to one hundred points. For smaller groups you may increase the point value of each activity.

Discussion Prompts
1. How do you feel after exercising?
2. Do you feel different emotionally?
3. How can exercise help you?
4. What do you do to exercise in your life right now?
5. What type of exercise could you do?
6. Was it easier to exercise with the challenge of the points?
7. What could you use for incentive to get you exercising now?

RESOURCE SCAVENGER HUNT

Free time can be spent doing activities that are negative or positive. Negative activities are things that are detrimental to a person's emotional well being. People who are depressed shouldn't sit at home alone if this adds to their depression. Someone who spends his/her free time in an environment of drugs, crime, or violent activity may need to find alternative ways of spending time.

The problem is that many people don't know what else they can do with their free time. This activity is a fun way to introduce people to the places they can go to find new and positive things they can do with their leisure time.

Objective
For people to recognize and find resources that can be used to help them locate and engage in appropriate recreational activities.

Who
People who need to expand and diversify the activities they engage in during their free time in order to create a healthier lifestyle for themselves.

Group Size
2 to 20 participants

Materials
- Several local phone books
- Stack of newspapers
- Pamphlets of events (found at your local Chamber of Commerce)

Description

Set all of the resources that you have available on a table and ask the group to gather around the table so that they all have access to the books, pamphlets and magazines. Inform the group that in this game their job is to get as many points as possible and the way to get points is to find anything that the leader names before someone else in the group finds it in the resources provided. The first one to find what is called out by the leader must raise his/her hand and show the group what s/he has found before the next item is called out.

1. Phone number of a city parks department
2. Name of a pizza place
3. A roller skating rink
4. Address of a chamber of commerce
5. Phone number of the library
6. The local YMCA or YWCA
7. Little League information
8. A movie that is playing at a local theater
9. A video store
10. As many parks as possible
11. A place with tennis courts
12. (Add to your list based upon the resources you have available)

Discussion Prompts

1. How do you usually find information on the activities you want to participate in?
2. What activities could you do in your daily life from the different things that you found in this activity?
3. What are some ways that you can find out about activities that you would like to pursue and become involved in?

Variation

⊃ May be done in teams, rather than individually.

LEiSURE BROCHURE

A brochure is a simple means of advertising that can get people excited about something new and fun. Many brochures are about recreational activities such as skiing, water slides, white water rafting, shopping, etc. The pictures and the words in the brochure are meant to spark your interest in the activity.

The leisure brochure activity is also an interest sparker. It is meant to get people interested in some of their old but forgotten activities and interest them in new things to fill their time.

Objective

For each person in the group to explore his/her own leisure interest, activity participation, and personal leisure lifestyle. To discuss how activity involvement can be used as a coping skill.

Who

People who spend their free time doing the same thing over and over again and who need to integrate a variety of activities, that can be used as coping mechanisms, into their lives.

Group Size

1 or more

Materials

- ➲ Paper
- ➲ Pens or pencils
- ➲ Colored markers, crayons or pencils
- ➲ Optional: Colored paper, scissors, glue, glitter, etc.

Description

If you have any brochures lying around that advertise activities and events (i.e. white water rafting, skiing and vacations and that can be found at your local Chamber of Commerce, outdoor stores, AAA, or travel agencies) bring them for the group to see, then talk about what a brochure is. A brochure is something that is used to advertise an activity, product or event and is used to get people interested in participating in all the fun that is described in its pages.

Ask everyone to create their own "leisure brochures" that advertises <u>all</u> of the interesting things they have done for fun and leisure in their life. The brochure should state why these are things the author enjoys and what is so great about each activity. The job of each person is to create a brochure that others will be interested in and that will create interest in the activities listed.

After everyone completes their brochure, allow time for sharing. This is a great way to get people to think about all the fun things they used to do but don't do anymore, to think about the things they enjoy doing now and to get new ideas for coping activities from others.

Discussion Prompts

1. Are there any activities that you thought of that you haven't done in a while but would like to do again? Why don't you?
2. How could any of the activities you listed help you to cope with your problems? Do you use these activities? If not, why?
3. Did you like any of the ideas someone else listed? If so, can you pursue any of these?

YOUR TIME

Sometimes you don't get to choose what you do with your time. At school your teacher chooses, at work your boss gives you your task for the day, and other times you simply have things that must be done as a part of everyday life. It is in your free time that you get to choose what you do, and during this time you have the power to improve your own life or the chance to make decisions that may have a negative impact on your life or on the lives of others. Making positive choices and understanding the power that comes with making these choices during your free time is what this activity is all about.

Objective
To help people to realize how they spend their free time and how they can change the way that they spend their free time to better enhance their own lives. To emphasize the power of choice when it comes to one's own free time.

Who
People who need to make better choices than they currently are making regarding how they spend their free time.

Group Size
3 to 10 is ideal

Materials
- ➲ Various game supplies
- ➲ A watch or timing device
- ➲ Question sheets (found on page 252)

Description
Divide the group time up so that each person is given an equal amount of time (i.e. if there are six people in the group and the group

time is an hour, then each person gets ten minutes). Each person decides which activity or game the group does for his/her allotted time, and the group must do this activity. Choices may be limited to the supplies available. Maybe one person wants to sing, another to play a card game, do crafts or play basketball. If these supplies are available, then the group will do all these different activities, one after another. Two people may choose the same game, and it will simply be played for twice as long.

Discussion Prompts

Ask each person to fill out the question sheet afterwards and then discuss the answers. Emphasize the feelings one gets from choosing his/her own activities and the importance of making healthy choices.

Your Time Question Sheet

1. How do you feel when <u>you</u> choose an activity and participate in it?

2. How do you feel when someone else chooses an activity for you?

3. What activities do you <u>choose</u> to participate in when you have free time?

4. Are these healthy activities? Why or why not?

5. Why is it important for you to spend your free time engaged in healthy activities?

PENCiL ME IN

Some people's lives are filled with constant activity, and they must keep a calendar just to keep track of their busy schedule, while others have lots of free time with nothing to do. People who are very busy may feel like they have no time for themselves and may become stressed and overwhelmed because they can't take time to relax. The person who has very little to do may become sad and depressed because they have limited chance to be in a social environment with others. If how you spend your free time needs to change, it may be a long process because old habits are hard to break, but this activity may give you the start that you need.

Objective
To help individuals to think about how they are spending their free time and to guide them in deciding if they need to make changes in order to improve their current lifestyles.

Who
People who need to schedule less in their free time to reduce stress. People who need to schedule more of their free time to help them become more social, interactive, and less depressed or lonely.

Group Size
1 or more

Materials
➲ Three copies of a blank weekly page from a day planner for each person.
➲ Pens or pencils

Description
Obtain a blank day planner or weekly calendar and make three

copies of one week for each person in the group (if this is not possible due to copyright infringement, or there is not one available, you may create a blank weekly calendar yourself). Give each person one copy and ask them to write down everything that they do during each day from the time they get up until they go to bed for a typical week (from Sunday to Saturday). After this task is completed, ask them to think about the choices they make and if there are any changes they wish they could make if they could plan a week filled with anything their hearts desired. Emphasize the importance of making healthy and positive choices during leisure time as a means of bettering one's own life and allow them to fill a second page with these new ideas.

After everyone has completed the second page discuss the differences found in what they usually do and what they would like to do. Now hand out the third sheet and ask each person to plan out the next week of his/her life. Ask them to fill the page with realistic ideas, but challenge them to do something different and to engage in as many healthy and positive activities as they can think of. Ask everyone to share what their plans are and if possible meet again at the end of the week to see if anyone has done anything different with their time as a result of this activity and what effect this had on their week and how they feel.

Discussion Prompts
(After the first sheet)
1. Do you feel like you are making healthy and positive choices with how you spend your free time?
2. What benefits could you gain in your life if you change how you spend your time?

(After second sheet)
1. Are these activities realistic?
2. Which activities are you most likely to pursue?
3. Why don't you do this now?
4. What would it take for you to change how you spend your free time?
5. How would it help you in your own life to pursue new activities?

(After third sheet)
1. Do you feel that you will follow through with your plan? Why or why not?

Variation

➲ Plan a week when working, when in school, when on vacation, a week with no TV and/or a week with extra spending money.

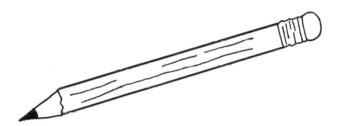

LIBRARY
SCAVENGER HUNT

Everybody knows that libraries offer books and are a great place to acquire knowledge, but people often overlook all the other great things offered by libraries and miss out on the great source of entertainment provided there. Today's libraries are filled with more than just books. Videos, music, computer access, magazines, newspapers, books about hobbies, and public services are all offered at many local libraries, and usually at no cost.

Once someone becomes familiar with the library system and all that it has to offer, they will be more willing to take advantage of all the benefits of their local library. A library scavenger hunt is a great way to introduce people to the wonderful treasures that can be found at your local library.

Objective
To learn more about a wonderful, community resource that is often overlooked. To learn how the library can be used to gain information about activities that can be used as coping skills.

Who
People who would benefit from using the resources available to them at their local library as a means of finding positive activities to engage in during their free time.

Group Size
1 or more

Materials
- 1 copy of the library scavenger hunt (found on pages 258-259, or create your own) per person
- Pens or pencils

Description

Prior to this activity go to your local library and create a list of the many different and interesting things that people can find there, look up, or locate. Each community library offers a variety of resources and most are similar in what they offer. The list found on the following pages was created from the materials found at my local library and you may add to it or subtract from it based upon what you find.

Take a field trip to the library with your group and give each person a pen or pencil and a copy of your library scavenger hunt list. Ask them to find the answers and to write them on the sheet. For added fun you may give a prize to anyone who completes the list or to the person who finishes first.

Discussion Prompts

1. Do you use the library often? Why or why not?
2. Did you find anything at the library that you didn't know they had? If so, what?
3. What can you get from the library besides books?
4. How can you utilize the library to help you fill your free time with healthy activities?

Library Scavenger Hunt

1. Find a story on audio cassette and write down the title:

   _____

2. For how many days can you check out an educational video?

   _____

3. Find a magazine title that begins with R.

   _____

4. Where is the California phone book located?

   _____

5. Give the title of a country CD found in the library.

   _____

6. Give the title of a book on How to Draw.

   _____

7. Find a magazine article on wind surfing and give the title of the article, the name of the magazine, issue and date.

   _____

8. Find a book with information about colleges in it.

    _____

9. Find a book on Italian cooking.

    _____

10. Find a book about your favorite sport.

    _____

11. Find an advertisement for a job that you would like to have someday (give the name of the job and source).

    _____

12. List 3 different computer resources found at the library.

    _____

13. Who can use the internet at the library?

    _____

14. What must you do in order to get a library card?

    _____

BONUS Find a book or article written by someone who has the same first or last name as you (list book or article and author).

    _____

FAMILY FUN TIMES

Some families do many things together while others just seem to live in the same house but don't do much together. Activities can build relationships among family members if everyone enjoys what the family is doing together. Sometimes people don't realize that they could be doing more with their families, and their family fun times (or lack of) need to be evaluated.

Objective
To encourage people to build relationships with their family members through leisure activities.

Group Size
1 or more

Who
People who could benefit from doing more activities with their family and who need to take a look at how their family spends their time together.

Materials
- Paper
- Pens or pencils

Description
Start the activity by asking each person to identify the people in their life that make up their family. For some people a family is obvious but for others it may be an aunt, uncle, grandparent, neighbor or even the people in their group home or foster family. After the group shares about their families, give each person a piece of paper and ask them to brainstorm and make a list of ten things their family enjoys doing together (anything from eating popcorn to going camping). Then ask

them to look at their list and to put different symbols by each activity.

$ - if the activity cost more than $10

→   - if you must go more than a 100 miles away for the activity

○   - if the activity brings your family closer together

☺   - if your family has done this in the last three months

Now circle your three favorite activities and think about what these activities say about your family values or lifestyle.

Discussion Prompts

1. What do these activities say about your family's values or lifestyle?
2. Do most of the activities require money?
3. Do you have to travel far for many of the activities?
4. Do the activities bring your family closer together?
5. Do you do activities with your family very much?
6. What things would you like to do with your family but don't do now? (you may add these to your list)
7. Why don't you do these activities? Would it be possible to do these activities?
8. How can doing things with your family help your relationship with your family members?

TAKE A TV BREAK

When there is nothing to do, it is easy to turn on the TV and become instantly entertained. Some people could benefit from spending their free time doing other things such as interacting with others or engaging in activities that build self-esteem or promote exercise. Helping people realize that they could benefit from doing things other than watching TV when there is nothing to do can be very helpful to those who need it.

Objective
To discuss the effect that TV has on people's lives and to think of alternative ways to spend one's time. To think of healthy, relationship building, life improvement activities that can be done during leisure time in the place of watching TV.

Who
People who spend too much of their free time watching TV, but who could benefit from engaging in social situations, educational activities, physical endeavors, or interactive activities.

Group Size
1 or more

Materials
- TV
- Video or TV show to watch
- Video recorder if needed
- Pens or pencils
- Two copies of the TV and Game Survey for each group member (found on page 264)
- Supplies to an interactive group game

Description

Select a TV show or video for the group to watch that you feel they might enjoy. Then have an interactive group game for the group to play such as cards, a board game, guessing game, or anything else that requires interaction. After playing the game ask everyone to fill out two different "TV and Game" surveys, one for the TV show and one for the game (you may have them fill out the TV show survey after watching the show and before playing the game). Gather the group together and talk about the differences between watching a TV show and playing an interactive game based upon the answers they gave to the questionnaires.

Discussion Prompts

After each survey discuss the answers that participants gave to each question. Talk about how much of their life and free time is filled with TV. At the end create a big group list of all the things someone can do during their free time (when they are bored) instead of watching TV.

Variation

⮑ This can be done with a solitary activity such as crafts, reading or cooking as well and compare the differences.

TV and Game Survey

1. How did you feel while watching this show or playing this game?

2. Did watching this video, or TV show or playing the game benefit you? If so, how?

3. Did this show or game have any negative effect on you, the group, or your relationship with others?

4. Do you ever watch TV just to be watching it or do you only watch the things that you choose ahead of time?

5. Do you ever feel like you waste your time when you watch TV?

6. Name as many activities as you can think of that you could do instead of watching TV when you are bored.

    (Use the back of this page if you need more room).

ALPHABETICAL LiST OF GAMES

THE wRECking YARD
OF GAMES AND ACTIVITIES

If you found *104 Activities That Build:* useful, helpful and informative, you'll love Alanna's other book – *The wRECking Yard of games and activities*!

The wRECking Yard contains 104 more games and activities that are unique, fun and therapeutic. The book covers the topics of teamwork, self-esteem, self-discovery, leisure education, communication, anger management, and fitness.

Teachers, counselors, therapist, and youth workers across the country have found this book to be a valuable resource that is quickly growing in popularity!

~ ISBN# 1-882883-35-7   246 pages   6"x9" ~

ADD 104 MORE GREAT ACTIVITIES TO YOUR COLLECTION FOR ONLY $24!!

(Order form found on last page of this book.)

TEAM UP

A new board game that you play with a team!

Team Up combines the fun of group initiatives, problem solving and teamwork activities with the simplicity of a creative new board game.

Can be played in small teams of three each or with a big group and teams as large as ten people each. Your team *must* work together each time it is your turn in order to win!

Team Up takes the outdoor adventure experience anywhere with a sturdy wooden game board that can be used out in a field, on a picnic table or even in a classroom.

Team Up comes with a game board, dice, playing pieces, therapeutic discussion sheets and 175 different activities that challenge any group - physically, mentally and individually to work for the good of the team.

This is a fun game for camp groups, therapy sessions, church groups, scouts and is great for use in any classroom. Any group that wants to grow closer together and learn by taking risk and by being challenged while at the same time laughing a lot and having fun will enjoy the game *Team Up*!!

<u>Ages:</u> 8 and up - <u>Number of players</u>: 6 to 60 - <u>Price</u>: $29

Team-Building Activities for Every Group

107 interactive games and activities can be found in the pages of this easy-to-use book. Each game is fun, experiential, easy to lead, unique, and requires minimal resources. With 65 team challenges and 42 activities that help any team get to know one another, become comfortable with each other, and open up, there is something for every group.

If you work with youth, corporate groups, therapy groups, church groups, scouts, families, school groups, sports teams, at camp, or with any other group who must work together you will find helpful games and activities in this fun, energetic, and purposeful book!

More Team-Building Activities for Every Group

More Team-Building Activities for Every Group contains 107 more games and activities that promote team-building in an interactive and fun way. The games are new, different, experiential, exciting, easy to lead and require minimal resources.

Find sample games from both books on our web site
www.gamesforgroups.com

(Order form found on last page of this book.)

Book and Game Order Form

TITLE	PRICE	QUANTITY	TOTAL
Team -Building Activities for	$16	_____	_____
More Team-Building Activities	$16	_____	_____
104 Activities That Build:	$24	_____	_____
The wRECking Yard	$24	_____	_____
Team Up (board game)	$29	_____	_____
Shipping: $4 (no matter how many items you order!)			_____

TOTAL [   ]

Name _____

Address _____

City _____ State _____ Zip_____

Telephone (_____)_____

Payment Type: Visa _____ Master Card_____Check _____ PO_____
Card number

_____

Expiration Date _____/_____ Name on card_____

Order by Fax, Phone or Mail to:
Rec Room Publishing
PO Box 2117
Lusby, MD 20657
Phone 1-888-325-GAME
Fax 1-888-530-GAME

Web Page: www.gamesforgroups.com